The Book On
Saying No

How to Take Back Your Time Without Burning Bridges

The Book On Series

Sage Monroe

Published by The Book On Publishing, 2025.
First edition. May 26, 2025.

Website: https://thebookon.ca
Substack: https://thebookonpublishing.substack.com/

SAYING NO: HOW TO TAKE BACK YOUR TIME WITHOUT BURNING BRIDGES

First edition. May 26, 2025.

Copyright © 2025 The Book On Publishing
ISBN: 978-1-997795-80-3

Written by Sage Monroe.

The Book On Series

Table of Contents

Read This First

This is not a book designed to entertain you. It's not here to charm, to soothe, or to hold your hand. It won't dazzle you with stories, metaphors, or motivational fluff. What you're having is a tool, an instruction manual written for people who are serious about learning, executing, and thinking at a higher level.

Every book in The Book On Series is built on a single premise: clarity beats complexity. We believe that when you strip away the noise, the emotions, the marketing spin, and the cultural rituals of "self-help," what's left is raw, unembellished instruction. That's what these books offer.

They are dry by design. Not because we don't care about language or narrative, but because when you're building something that matters, you don't need more distractions. You need a clear architecture. Mental scaffolding. Direction that respects your intelligence.

Each title in this series takes on a specific domain: decision-making, clarity, strategy, leverage, and uncertainty, and drills deep. Not in sweeping generalizations, but in applied frameworks. These are books for builders, operators, founders, tacticians, and thinkers, people who don't just consume knowledge but operationalize it.

You'll find no chapter-long anecdotes here. No self-congratulatory memoirs. No bullet-point platitudes. Instead, what you'll get is structured insight: argument, example, application. The tone is direct. The prose is sober. The ideas are designed to be lifted out and used.

You won't be coddled, but you won't be misled either.

There's a place in the world for lyrical, emotional, story-driven books, and this isn't that place. This is a workspace. A blueprint. A conversation for people who are ready to act, not just absorb.

We respect your time and your intellect.

Welcome to The Book On Series.

Introduction

Saying no is one of the most straightforward yet most powerful acts of self-care and self-respect. Yet, for many of us, it can feel impossibly difficult, a source of guilt, anxiety, and second-guessing. We live in a world that rewards compliance, politeness, and the willingness to put others first, often at the expense of our own needs and boundaries. This habit of saying yes, sometimes out of fear, habit, or obligation, can quietly erode our time, energy, and sense of self.

The Book on Saying No: How to Take Back Your Time Without Burning Bridges is your guide to breaking free from this cycle. It is a compassionate invitation to reclaim your voice, your time, and your life by learning the art of saying no, without guilt, without fear, and without burning the bridges that matter.

This book explores the deep cultural, psychological, and emotional reasons we struggle to say no. It uncovers the invisible costs of constant agreement: the exhaustion, resentment, and lost opportunities that often go unnoticed. But more than that, it offers practical tools and strategies, clear language, boundary-setting skills, and mindset shifts that empower you to set limits confidently and kindly.

Saying no is not about shutting others out; it's about creating space for what truly matters. It is an act of kindness toward yourself and those around you. When you learn to say no with compassion and clarity, you open the door to saying yes to your highest priorities, your well-being, and your authentic life.

Whether you are exhausted from people-pleasing, overwhelmed at work, or struggling to set boundaries in personal relationships, this book will guide you step by step. It offers stories, reflections, exercises, and scripts designed to meet you where you are and help you move toward a freer, more balanced way of living.

Your journey to reclaiming your time and your power begins here. You deserve to live a life shaped by choice, not obligation, a life where your no is honored as much as your yes. Welcome to the first step.

- Sage Monroe

Dedication

To everyone who has ever felt overwhelmed by the weight of saying yes when their heart whispered no, may this book be a gentle guide toward reclaiming your voice, your time, and your freedom.

To those who dare to set boundaries with courage and kindness, even when it feels challenging or uncertain, your strength lights the way.

And to the countless invisible workers, caretakers, and people-pleasers whose generosity deserves to be honored and protected, this is for you.

-    Sage Monroe

Chapter 1: The Yes Trap, How We Got Here

The Quiet Curriculum of Compliance

From the moment we begin to form language, we are taught that "yes" is good. "Say yes to your grandmother." "Say yes when someone offers help." "Yes, teacher." "Yes, coach." "Yes, boss." The word flows easily, polished by repetition, rewarded with smiles and approval. It becomes more than a word; it becomes a key to acceptance. For many of us, especially those raised in environments where politeness and obedience were prized above individuality, the habit of saying yes was woven into the fabric of our character before we even knew we had a choice.

This early training is not overtly malicious. It's usually born from a desire to raise respectful, cooperative children. But the unintended consequence is a generation, or several, of adults who equate "no" with rudeness, rebellion, or rejection. We internalize the belief that to be kind is to be accommodating, that to be liked we must be available, and that turning someone down risks turning them against us. Saying no becomes emotionally expensive.

The social script is subtle but relentless: be helpful, be flexible, be agreeable. This programming intensifies based on gender, culture, and family dynamics. Girls, in particular, are often taught to be pleasant and compliant, to avoid being "bossy" or "difficult." Boys may be allowed more assertiveness, but even they aren't immune to the pull of performance and approval, especially when it comes to authority. Across all identities, the message is clear: don't rock the boat.

Over time, the reward loop gets entrenched. Say yes, get liked. Say yes, avoid conflict. Say yes, earn praise. By the time we reach adulthood, "yes" feels like a survival strategy. It smooths over tension, cements our belonging, and gives us a sense of usefulness. But beneath that comfort is a growing cost. Every yes that isn't aligned with our true desires erodes a bit of our time, energy, and identity.

Saying no, by contrast, feels risky. It challenges our conditioning. It forces us to stand alone, even briefly. It opens the door to disappointment, to potential backlash, to being misunderstood. And yet, the inability to say no is not without its dangers. The longer we live in default yes-mode, the further we drift from our own needs and priorities. The further we drift, the harder it becomes to hear the inner voice that says: Enough.

Invisible Labor and Emotional Expense

In personal relationships and professional environments alike, saying yes too often quietly signs us up for invisible labor. This labor takes many forms: managing emotions in a conversation, taking on extra tasks at work without recognition, being the friend who always listens, the family member who always hosts, the employee who always stays late. These contributions rarely show up on a to-do list, let alone a paycheck, but they extract real energy and time.

Invisible labor is especially insidious because it's socially reinforced. We rarely get asked, "Do you have the bandwidth for this emotional burden?" Instead, we get praise for being dependable, selfless, or strong. But strength becomes a trap when it's defined by how much you can carry rather than how clearly you can say no. The more we say yes, the more is expected. The more we deliver, the more invisible our effort becomes. And the cycle deepens.

The emotional toll of chronic compliance can be hard to quantify, but it shows up in the body and the soul. Fatigue, irritability, low-level resentment, a creeping sense of being used or unseen; these are the symptoms of a boundary system left unattended. When we're constantly reacting to external requests and expectations, we rarely get a chance to ask ourselves what we truly want or what's best for us. Life becomes a performance in service of others, and our storyline fades into the background.

This pattern doesn't arise in a vacuum. Cultural narratives play a decisive role. Western society, in particular, glorifies hustle and helpfulness. We celebrate the self-made entrepreneur who works 80 hours a week, the mother who sacrifices everything for her children, and the employee who never takes a sick day. These images create a blueprint for what a "good" life looks like: full, busy, helpful to others. Rest becomes laziness. Saying no becomes selfishness.

But beneath the surface, more people than ever are feeling the strain. Mental health crises, burnout rates, and disconnection from self are on the rise. Many of us live with a constant, low-grade anxiety that something is wrong, not necessarily with the world, but with our place in it. We're overextended, undernourished, and unsure how to change. We feel guilty for being tired, guilty for wanting more, guilty for saying no. So, we keep saying yes.

Until something breaks.

Cultural Inheritance and Generational Shifts

Every generation inherits a set of rules for how to behave, how to connect, and how to contribute. Many of these rules are unwritten but deeply felt. They shape how we show up in the world. For Baby Boomers, saying yes was often tied to duty and loyalty. Their upbringing, steeped in post-war values, emphasized responsibility to family, job security, and community cohesion. Sacrifice was noble; individual needs were secondary. Saying no could be seen as ungrateful or rebellious, a threat to order and tradition.

Generation X brought some skepticism to these inherited ideals. Often caught between the rigidity of Boomer values and the looming pressures of a changing economic landscape, Gen Xers began to question the cost of always conforming. Yet many still carried forward the belief that you prove your worth through perseverance and independence. Saying no felt like dropping the ball, even if you were carrying far too many.

Millennials inherited a different kind of pressure: to be everything to everyone, all the time. Raised in the shadow of the self-esteem movement and the advent of the internet, they were told they could do anything and often internalized that as needing to do everything. With work and social life increasingly blending into one stream of notifications and obligations, saying yes became both a habit and a trap. Millennial burnout isn't just about long hours; it's about the impossibility of meeting countless, conflicting expectations.

Then came Gen Z, who are rewriting the script in real time. More attuned to mental health, more skeptical of traditional work structures, and more fluent in the language of boundaries, Gen Z is beginning to model a new paradigm. They're quicker to say no, quicker to opt out of systems that don't serve them. They understand, perhaps more innately, that saying no is a survival skill in a world that constantly demands your attention, your output, your consent.

Still, the shift isn't complete. Most of us, regardless of age, are straddling two worlds: the one that shaped us and the one we want to shape. We feel the pull of old scripts and the promise of new ones. And between those poles lies discomfort. Growth. Resistance. But also, the chance to choose again.

Learning to say no isn't just about modern self-care. It's about reclaiming authorship of your life. It's about recognizing the invisible architecture of social rules and choosing which ones to keep. It's about breaking intergenerational patterns that no longer serve us and forging new paths rooted in alignment, not obligation. And that begins with noticing where the yeses are automatic, and asking, finally, whether they should be.

The Psychological Roots of People-Pleasing

To understand why saying no feels so hard, we must go deeper into the psychological roots of our need to please. For many, this behavior isn't merely learned; it's a survival mechanism. As children, we depend on the approval and attention of caregivers for safety and belonging. If we experienced love as conditional, based on good behavior, academic performance, and emotional containment, then pleasing became a way to secure our place in the family system.

This pattern extends into adulthood. People-pleasing becomes a strategy to avoid abandonment, conflict, or disapproval. It's often driven by a fear that being fully yourself, expressing needs, preferences, or limits, will result in rejection. So instead, you edit. You adapt. You say yes, even when you mean no. You smile when you're hurting. You offer help when you're overwhelmed. And slowly, you lose track of where others end, and you begin.

This blurring of self is subtle but pervasive. It shows up in everyday decisions: agreeing to plans you dread, staying silent when something hurts, bending your schedule to fit someone else's priorities. It can even disguise itself as generosity or empathy. But genuine empathy does not require self-erasure. It does not demand that you betray yourself to avoid disappointing someone else.

The irony is that people-pleasing rarely creates the deep connection we crave. It often leads to imbalance, resentment, and disconnection, not only from others, but from ourselves. We become actors in our own lives, playing the role of the agreeable one, the strong one, the caretaker. Meanwhile, our inner world contracts, leaving little space for desire, rest, or truth.

Reclaiming your no requires facing the discomfort that comes with letting go of that role. It requires unlearning the belief that your worth is tied to usefulness, performance, or likability. And it demands the courage to be seen not as perfect or agreeable, but as whole.

The path back to yourself begins with a single, radical act: telling the truth about what you want. And that truth often starts with no.

Invisible Labor and the High Price of Being Agreeable

Invisible labor refers to the unseen effort behind the scenes, encompassing emotional, logistical, and energetic work that often goes unnoticed and unappreciated. It's organizing the birthday party no one thanked you for, remembering dietary preferences, adjusting your schedule around everyone else's, staying silent to keep the peace, smoothing over social awkwardness, or offering emotional support when no one asked if *you* were okay. For many, especially women and people raised with nurturing expectations, this labor becomes habitual, so ingrained that it feels less like a choice and more like a default setting.

This kind of unpaid, unspoken effort doesn't show up on timesheets or tax returns, but it accumulates in the nervous system like emotional debt. Over time, the small "yeses" stack up. Yes, I'll make the call. Yes, I'll reschedule. Yes, I'll let it go. Yes, I'll help again, even though I'm tired. And eventually, those yeses start to exact a toll not just on time and energy, but on one's very sense of self.

Agreeableness becomes a mask we forget we're wearing. It was once a strategy, a way to be safe, to feel needed, to avoid rejection. But somewhere along the way, we internalize the idea that it's who we are. When we say "I just like to help" or "I'm easygoing," what we often mean is "I've learned it's safer to absorb discomfort than to cause it."

And yet, even those who pride themselves on being helpful and reliable begin to feel the quiet sting of imbalance. Resentment, though often buried under layers of rationalization, starts to surface. You begin to notice the one-sidedness of certain relationships. The expectation that you will stretch, flex, and accommodate becomes so routine that no one sees it as a compromise anymore; it's just who you are to them. But what about who you are to *you*?

This is where chronic compliance becomes not just a behavioral issue, but a question of identity. How do you know what you want if you've spent years making decisions based on what will keep the waters calm? How do you identify your valid preferences when the reflex to accommodate takes over before your own needs even register?

What's even more complicated is that invisible labor is often socially rewarded. You're called dependable, caring, and a team player. These are admirable qualities, no doubt, but they become weaponized when they're expected without limit. The moment you pause or resist, the script flips. You're suddenly "not being supportive," "difficult," or "not like you." The praise that once felt like fuel now becomes pressure.

The expectations that others hold of us are often mirrors of what we have tolerated in ourselves. If you've always been the one who says yes, people will continue to expect it, not out of malice, but because patterns become invisible the longer they're sustained. It's not just about re-educating others, it's about waking yourself up to what you've agreed to, and why.

This moment of awakening is uncomfortable. It requires admitting that what once felt like generosity may have been people-pleasing. That what you thought was kindness may have been fear. That your most applauded traits have come at a personal cost you can no longer afford to pay.

And yet, this reckoning is also liberating.

Because once you see the patterns, you can start to change them. You can begin to question the automatic yes. You can sit with the discomfort of possibly letting someone down and realize you'll survive it. You can test the waters of boundaries and find, to your surprise, that the world doesn't end when you say no; it often begins.

But before that liberation comes into focus, there's grief. Grief for the time lost, the opportunities passed over, the exhaustion endured in silence. Grief for the parts of yourself you had to tuck away to be palatable. And perhaps most bittersweet, grief for the self you never got to be because you were too busy being what others needed.

This is not a sad story, though. It's a turning point. A moment where you stop asking how to be less of a burden and start asking how to be more of *yourself.* Where you shift from constantly managing others' emotions to becoming more responsible for your own.

But change, even necessary change, can feel threatening to the status quo. Not just externally, in your relationships, but internally too. Your nervous system is wired for familiarity. Saying no may feel like danger because it's unknown, not because it's wrong. That's why simply having the *desire* to say no is a radical act. It means a deeper part of you is ready, ready to reclaim time, energy, voice, and identity.

And yet, readiness doesn't always feel like confidence. It might feel like shakiness, like doubt, like guilt. That's okay. Confidence is not the prerequisite for change; commitment is. The commitment to explore, to stumble, to try again. To begin honoring the small voice within that says, "Enough."

As we approach the close of this first chapter, let's take a breath. You've come by your patterns honestly. There is no shame in having learned to survive by saying yes. Many of us have been trained to equate safety with compliance, acceptance with self-abandonment, and belonging with silence. You did what you had to do. And now, if you're reading this, you may be ready to do something else.

The good news? You don't have to do it alone. This book is not a lecture or a list of hacks; it's a companion for the journey. A compassionate guide through the messy, exhilarating, awkward, and freeing process of learning to say no, not as a weapon, but as a truth. A truth that frees you, even as it may challenge others.

In the next segment, we'll bring this chapter to a close by synthesizing what we've uncovered so far and preparing you for the chapters ahead. Because learning to say no isn't just about communication, it's about transformation.

Reclaiming the Self

You're not here because you don't care about others. You're here because you've cared so deeply, so often, that the balance has quietly tipped from compassion to depletion. You're here because you've begun to suspect that there's more to life than keeping the peace. Because you've heard a whisper, sometimes in your body, in your thoughts, that says, *This isn't working anymore.*

That whisper is not a weakness. It's the truth. It's the voice of the self you've muted in service of smoothness, likability, harmony, and survival. It's the part of you that's been watching all along while you said yes when you meant no, smiled when you wanted to leave, and offered when you had nothing left to give. And now, finally, it's starting to speak louder.

And still, there may be doubt. "Is it really okay to say no?" "What if I hurt someone?" "What if I change too much and people don't understand me anymore?"

These questions are entirely valid. You've spent years, maybe decades, learning to navigate your world through compliance. You've learned that it's safer to accommodate than to confront, to absorb discomfort rather than hand it back. You've been praised for it, depended on for it, even loved for it. But love that depends on your erasure isn't love. It's a transaction. It's roleplay. It's an arrangement you didn't know you were making until it started to choke you.

That's why saying no can feel so personal. It doesn't just disrupt an interaction; it disrupts a whole identity. Who are you if not the helper, the fixer, the easy one, the reliable one, the always-there-for-everyone-but-yourself one? It's a terrifying question. But it's also the doorway to something real.

You are not your role. You are not your usefulness. You are not obligated to perpetuate a self-sacrificing version of yourself just because others have come to rely on it. You are allowed to grow. You are allowed to disappoint others. You are permitted to be misunderstood. And most importantly, you are allowed to protect your peace without apology.

Saying no is the start of remembering who you were before the world told you who to be. It's how you reclaim time not just on your calendar, but in your life. It's how you begin to make decisions rooted in desire instead of fear. It's how you reconnect with your body, your intuition, your purpose, not as abstract concepts, but as daily realities. Not everything can come with you into the next chapter. Not every relationship will survive your boundaries. Not every dynamic can be salvaged once you stop playing your assigned role. But what you'll gain in return is priceless.

You'll gain space. You'll gain clarity. You'll gain energy you didn't know you had because it was being siphoned off by constant over-giving. And slowly, you'll gain a sense of self that is not conditional, one that does not rely on being liked, needed, or convenient.

The road to that self is not always smooth. But it is sacred. And like any journey worth taking, it requires preparation, guidance, and the courage to walk forward even when the path isn't obvious. This book is your guide. Not a rulebook, not a manifesto, but a grounded, practical, emotionally honest invitation back to yourself.

In the chapters ahead, we'll examine what's truly at stake when you say yes out of fear rather than alignment. We'll discuss the costs, both emotional, physical, financial, and spiritual, of chronic overcommitment. We'll redefine what it means to be kind, to be generous, to be in community, without losing your center. We'll build the inner and outer language for boundaries. We'll navigate workplace politics, family guilt, friendship expectations, and the trickiest frontier of all, saying no to *yourself* when you're tempted to overdo, overprove, or over function.

Each chapter will be both a mirror and a map. You'll be asked to reflect, not to ruminate. To practice, not just to ponder. To confront some of the more profound truths beneath your default yes, not to judge yourself, but to free yourself.

And through it all, you'll begin to feel a shift. Maybe not dramatic at first. Perhaps just a bit of breath in your lungs when you turn down something that used to be a reflexive yes. A little more time at the end of your day that feels like yours again. A little more peace in your chest when you don't explain yourself to someone who didn't earn that access.

This is the beginning of the end of over-giving. Not because giving is wrong, but because giving without boundaries is unsustainable. You are not here to be used up. You are here to live, love, rest, create, connect, and exist with wholeness. That starts with learning to say no, not just once, not just perfectly, but regularly, imperfectly, and with heart.

Let this be your permission slip. Not because you needed one, but because it helps to have it in writing:

➢ You are allowed to say no.
➢ You are allowed to need rest, solitude, boundaries, and space.

- ➢ You are allowed to disappoint others without betraying yourself.
- ➢ You are allowed to change.
- ➢ You are allowed to take your life back.

Now that we've explored the roots of our difficulty with saying no, how socialization and deep-seated patterns shape our responses, it's vital to turn our attention to the tangible consequences of these patterns. What does it cost us to keep saying yes? Chapter 2 delves into the often invisible toll on our time, energy, and well-being, laying bare the price of chronic compliance.

Let's begin.

Chapter 2: The Slow Burn of Yes

It rarely starts with a catastrophe. Saying yes too often usually begins innocently, an extra task here, a small favor there, a spontaneous commitment on a Tuesday afternoon that wasn't in your plan but felt too awkward to refuse. No alarms sound. No dramatic fallout. Just the subtle feeling of being slightly more tired, slightly more stretched, somewhat more out of sync with yourself.

But over time, the weight accumulates. One yes blends into the next, and the calendar fills not with priorities but with obligations. Days begin to feel dictated, your schedule overrun by needs that are not your own. This is the slow burn of yes. It doesn't announce itself. It wears you down by degrees. And by the time most people realize the cost, it's because they've already paid more than they meant to.

We tend to think of "burnout" as something that happens only to high-powered professionals or people with visibly demanding roles. But the truth is, burnout is democratic. It doesn't care if you're a CEO or a stay-at-home parent, an overcommitted college student, or a friend who can't stop showing up for everyone but themselves. Burnout is not always about working too hard; it's about giving more than you have, for longer than you can afford to.

The consequences of chronic over-agreement aren't just psychological, they're physiological. You feel it in your bones, your breath, your digestion, your sleep. The nervous system doesn't distinguish between work stress and boundary violations; it simply registers that you're overwhelmed and under-supported.

You may wake up exhausted, struggle to focus, and feel on edge with no apparent cause. Your body keeps the score, even when your mind insists, *I should be able to handle this.*

This internal conflict, between what your body is signaling and what your mind is rationalizing, is where so many people get stuck. They feel the drain, the fatigue, the dread. But they also feel guilt at the thought of pulling back. The idea of saying no feels not just tricky, but disloyal. So, they continue. They agree to the project that will disrupt their weekend, the dinner that will cost them the evening of quiet they craved, and the favor that depletes their limited energy reserves. And still, they tell themselves they're just being "helpful," "generous," "good."

But what if the generosity that costs you your well-being isn't generous?

What if saying yes to everything doesn't make you a good person, it just makes you an exhausted one?

The truth is, there are consequences for constantly overextending yourself, and they often surface long before you're willing to admit what's happening. They show up in the form of irritability, snapping at loved ones for minor things. They show up as emotional numbing, scrolling your phone endlessly, procrastinating, or zoning out in meetings and conversations. They show up as creative depletion, projects that once excited you now feel burdensome. And eventually, they show up as disconnection, not just from others, but from yourself.

You stop knowing what you want, because you're too busy meeting what everyone else wants. You lose clarity on your priorities because they've been shaped around others' needs. You become a composite of your responsibilities, navigating a life that appears functional but feels hollow.

This is the cost of saying yes too much: the quiet erosion of your own life.

Of course, some yeses are necessary. Life is full of collaboration, sacrifice, and interdependence. This is not a call for isolation or hyper-individualism. But there's a chasm between intentional giving and compulsive agreement. The former is rooted in choice. The latter, in fear.

And fear, left unchecked, will run your life in a thousand subtle ways. Fear of missing out. Fear of being replaced. Fear of seeming selfish. Fear of losing connection. These fears often masquerade as duty, as obligation, as "doing the right thing." But the body knows the difference. The body knows when you're living out of alignment. The body knows when every yes is a small self-betrayal. And eventually, that knowledge turns into symptoms.

You might notice you're more tired, even after rest. More anxious, even when there's no immediate threat. You may feel less tolerant of small talk, more sensitive to noise, and increasingly detached from your joy. These are not just quirks. They are data points. They are signs.

And if you ignore them for long enough, your body will find louder ways to get your attention. Panic attacks. Digestive issues. Sleep disorders. Fatigue that no amount of coffee can fix. This isn't alarmism, it's a fact. The human system was not built for constant acquiescence. You cannot keep overriding your limits without consequence.

But even as the body protests, the mind resists change. Many of us have internalized the belief that our worth is tied to our output. That our value is measured in sacrifice. That being helpful is what makes us lovable. These beliefs are not incidental; they are survival strategies. They've kept us connected, included, and affirmed. And so, the idea of changing, of saying no, doesn't feel like a shift in behavior. It feels like an identity risk.

And yet, something in you knows it's time.

Not because you've failed. Not because you're broken. But because your life is too meaningful to be spent on automatic yeses. Because your time is too precious to be treated like an open buffet. Because your health, your relationships, and your dreams all depend on your ability to protect your resources.

Saying no isn't just a skill. It's a recalibration of your entire way of being in the world. It's a reckoning with the belief that you have to earn your place, that your needs are secondary, that your worth is tied to your usefulness. Saying no is how you interrupt that belief. It's how you begin to reclaim not just your time, but your autonomy.

This chapter will take you further into that reclamation. We'll look at specific domains where chronic yes-ing does damage, including your energy, relationships, creativity, and even your finances. We'll examine real-life stories of people who agreed their way into collapse and what it took for them to recover. And we'll invite you to begin your inquiry, not with judgment, but with honesty.

Because nothing changes until we're willing to tell the truth.

The Hidden Tax of Time and Energy

Time is one of the only non-renewable resources you have. Once it's gone, it's gone. And yet, we give it away more freely than almost anything else. Sometimes, we care deeply about people. Often to those we barely know. And far too often, to tasks, events, or obligations that barely register on our scale of meaning but loom large on someone else's.

You likely know the feeling: that flinch of regret after agreeing to something you didn't honestly want to do. The mental math you perform as you stare at a calendar square filled with things you promised to attend or accomplish, not because you were inspired, but because you didn't want to make waves. The quiet resentment that builds as you realize your week has been shaped by someone else's needs, priorities, and pace.

This is the hidden tax of saying yes. You may not feel it immediately, but the interest compounds. Each small concession takes a sliver of your time and energy. On their own, these slivers seem manageable. But they rarely come alone. The dinner you agreed to out of obligation also costs you the hour of transition beforehand when you're mentally preparing, the time spent in traffic, and the depleted state you come home in. The "quick favor" for a coworker can divert your focus from finishing your project, causing it to spill over into your evening as you try to catch up.

What looks like a single yes is often five or six small sacrifices stacked together. And when you say yes repeatedly throughout your week, without reflection, without boundaries, without consideration, you don't just lose time. You lose momentum. You lose mental clarity. You lose the energy needed to do your best work or be fully present with those who matter most.

Many people don't realize the full extent of this cost until they attempt something that requires sustained attention and creative focus. A writing project, a business idea, a personal goal. They sit down to dive deep and discover... nothing. They're exhausted before they begin. Their tank is empty, not because they're lazy or unmotivated, but because they've bled energy in a thousand small, unaccounted-for directions.

Creative energy doesn't thrive in overcommitted lives. It needs space. It needs stillness. It needs a margin. And most importantly, it needs sovereignty, an intact sense of *your* direction and desires. When you spend most of your day responding instead of initiating, reacting instead of choosing, you lose access to that sovereignty. You become, in effect, a service provider for everyone else's priorities.

This is not a call to become selfish or self-absorbed. But it *is* a call to become aware. Because without awareness, you cannot discern. And without discernment, your yes is meaningless; it's just a reflex.

There's also a more insidious effect of this overextension: it erodes your sense of control. When your days are filled with tasks that don't reflect your values or goals, you begin to feel like life is happening *to* you, rather than *through* you. Even if you're technically "doing the right thing," it doesn't feel satisfying; it feels like maintenance. You're keeping up appearances, checking boxes, fulfilling expectations. But joy? Purpose? Momentum?

Those things require alignment, and alignment requires boundaries.

One of the most liberating things you can do is reclaim your yes by clarifying your no. The clearer your boundaries, the more powerful your yes becomes, not just in theory, but in how it shapes your time. You begin to reserve energy for what truly matters: deep connection, meaningful work, genuine rest, and creative exploration. You stop hemorrhaging energy on obligations that don't nourish or fulfill you.

This shift doesn't require a total life overhaul. It begins with a pause. A breath. A moment of reflection before the automatic yes. It starts by distinguishing between commitments you've chosen and those that were inherited, imposed, or assumed. It begins with asking, *If I weren't afraid of disappointing someone, what would I say?*

That question alone can reveal your true nature.

It's also important to recognize that not all overcommitment is external. Many people create their own overwhelm by over-scheduling, overpromising, or over-functioning, often in an attempt to prove something. To feel needed. To avoid stillness, which can feel like emptiness if you've tied your worth to your output. This is where the emotional cost of saying yes too often intersects with deeper psychological patterns: perfectionism, codependency, imposter syndrome, or unresolved trauma.

In these cases, it's not just about learning to say no to others; it's about learning to say no to the compulsive voice inside that equates rest with laziness, space with uselessness, or boundaries with failure. It's about unhooking your identity from the idea that

31

your value is determined by how much you do or how many people you please.

Saying no, then, becomes not just a boundary-setting act; it becomes a healing act. Each no is a thread in the larger work of repairing your relationship with yourself. Each no makes space for a deeper yes, yes to health, yes to presence, yes to work that lights you up, yes to relationships that don't require self-betrayal.

But before those yeses can take root, something else must happen. You have to be willing to see the cost of your current patterns. Not just the occasional inconvenience, but the long-term toll: the emotional fatigue, the stalled dreams, the resentment you don't talk about, the version of yourself that gets buried under everyone else's needs.

This is not about blame. It's about clarity. When you see the whole picture and begin to connect the dots between your chronic tiredness, foggy focus, creative stagnation, and simmering frustration, you can start to reclaim your agency. You can begin to recognize that every yes has a price, and that price is paid in the currency of your life.

Time. Energy. Focus. Presence. These are not abstract concepts. They are the architecture of your days. And your days, over time, become your life.

It's not too late to shift.

In the next segment, we'll explore how overcommitment not only costs you time and energy but can also destabilize your relationships, particularly when they're based on a pattern of one-sided giving. The emotional cost of saying yes too often runs deeper than most people realize, and understanding this can be the first step toward a more honest, balanced connection.

Resentment in Disguise

We tend to associate kindness with sacrifice, especially in close relationships. We want to be there for the people we care about. We want to show up, lend a hand, and go the extra mile. But without boundaries, what starts as generosity can quietly morph into obligation, and from obligation into resentment. And unlike anger, resentment doesn't announce itself with volume or clarity. It simmers. It leaks. It twists your perception of people you once loved, showing up for.

You begin to interpret their requests as demands. Their needs feel like intrusions. Their presence begins to exhaust you, even when they haven't done anything overtly wrong. Why? Because deep down, part of you is keeping score, even if you hate that you're doing it.

This is one of the most painful and rarely discussed outcomes of chronic over-giving: the erosion of genuine intimacy. When you say yes too often, especially when you don't mean it, you start to relate to others not through presence, but through performance. You're playing a role, one that looks generous on the surface, but under it all, you're exhausted, maybe even angry, but unsure how to voice it without upsetting the balance.

The tragedy is that many people who struggle to say no are profoundly relational. They care deeply and instinctively. But when every interaction becomes a test of endurance or an exercise in self-suppression, real closeness becomes impossible. You can't be truly intimate with someone when you're constantly editing yourself to avoid conflict or disappointment. The relationship might survive, but only in a hollowed-out form.

This dynamic shows up in friendships, families, romantic partnerships, and even in professional mentorships. Consider the friend who always listens but never shares. The partner who says yes to every chore, every errand, every plan, but grows more distant over time. The parent who meets every need with a smile until they explode in exhaustion, confusing everyone who didn't know how close they were to the edge.

One of the biggest myths we carry is that saying yes will keep the peace. In truth, peace cannot exist where truth is suppressed. There may be quiet. There may be agreement. But beneath the surface, there's tension, and that tension eventually finds a way out, often at the worst possible time.

The suppressed noise doesn't disappear. It festers. It turns into passive-aggressive behavior, sarcasm, withdrawal, or sudden anger. It damages trust because the people around you don't know where you stand. They don't know what you need, what you can handle, or what you're silently enduring. You haven't given them a chance to support your boundaries because you haven't made them visible.

This creates a dynamic where others unknowingly benefit from your silence, while you quietly suffer from their ignorance. But the blame doesn't fall solely on them; it's a co-created pattern. You've trained them to expect your compliance, and they've adapted accordingly. Changing this dynamic isn't about confrontation; it's about correction. Realignment. It's about inviting honesty back into the relationship.

When you start saying no after initially saying yes, some people will be surprised. Others may be hurt, confused, or even defensive. This is natural. You're disrupting a rhythm that has been beneficial to them, whether consciously or not. But you're also offering them something more valuable than your unending availability: the truth.

Not everyone will accept that truth with grace. Some will push back. Some may drift away. But those who remain, those who respect your new clarity, will be relating to the real you, not the agreeable version you've presented out of fear or habit.

It's worth asking yourself this: Do I want connection based on my boundaries, or my ability to override them?

It's a difficult question. Mainly, if your sense of belonging has long depended on how agreeable or helpful you are, but this is the turning point. Because while it may feel like you're risking connection by saying no, the opposite is often true. You're risking a false connection in exchange for the possibility of something real.

This shift can also bring up grief. You may realize certain relationships were never as mutual as you believed. That your role was always to serve, to soothe, to support, but never to ask, to decline, or to disappoint. You may find that once you stop over-functioning, the dynamic falls apart. And while that may feel like a loss, it's clarity.

Genuine relationships don't require self-abandonment. Real love doesn't demand silence in the face of discomfort. Mutual respect includes the ability to say no without fear of emotional exile.

But again, change begins with awareness. The resentment you feel isn't something to be ashamed of; it's a signal. It's telling you where the energy leak is, where you're giving more than you have. Where your yes is no longer sacred but expected.

Resentment is not a failure of generosity. It's the inevitable outcome of generosity that's been disconnected from truth.

So, how do you repair a relationship that's been shaped by chronic yeses? You start by being honest with yourself first, and then, when you're ready, with the other person. You name the pattern. You take responsibility for your part. You express what's changing and why. Not to accuse or blame, but to clarify and reconnect.

"I've realized I've been saying yes to things I don't always have the bandwidth for, and I want to start being more honest with myself and others."

"I value our relationship, and I want to show up in ways that feel sustainable and mutual. That means sometimes I'll need to say no when I would've said yes in the past."

"I've been noticing some resentment on my end, and I don't want that to affect how I show up with you. I need to make a few changes so I can stay in integrity."

These are not confrontations, they're invitations. And while they may not always be received perfectly, they plant a seed. They open a door. And over time, they create space for relationships built on choice rather than obligation.

In the next segment, we'll shift to another area where the hidden cost of over-yes-ing reveals itself: your finances and sense of value. Because how you use your time isn't just about energy, it's also about how you price, prioritize, and protect the most valuable asset you have: yourself.

The Financial Fallout of the Default: Yes

Most people don't consider people-pleasing a financial issue. It seems like a matter of time, stress, or maybe emotional labor. But the more closely you examine the behaviors surrounding chronic agreement, the unpaid favors, the volunteer hours, the undervalued work, the more you'll see the economic consequences.

Time *is* money. Energy *is* money. And every time you say yes out of fear, guilt, or obligation, you're not just spending emotional currency, you're giving away financial power.

Take, for example, the professional who consistently says yes to "just one more thing" at work. Whether it's staying late, absorbing tasks that aren't in their job description, or taking on a colleague's responsibilities to be a "team player," that person is doing more labor than they're being paid for. And if that pattern continues unchecked, it doesn't just affect their energy; it affects their earnings. Over-functioners rarely advocate for raises. People-pleasers don't always negotiate. And when your default mode is to accommodate, you may not even notice when your skills are being exploited rather than recognized.

This dynamic extends beyond the office. Freelancers and business owners who struggle to say no often find themselves undercharging, overdelivering, and constantly revising their boundaries in hopes of retaining clients or keeping relationships pleasant. They give discounts where they shouldn't. They answer calls on weekends. They scope-creep themselves into exhaustion. All because the discomfort of potentially disappointing someone outweighs the pain of being overworked and underpaid.

But here's the truth: when you consistently say yes to unpaid labor, discounted rates, or extra favors, you're training people to expect your devaluation.

It's not just about numbers. It's about the story behind the numbers, what you believe you're worth, what you feel you're allowed to ask for, and whether you think standing up for that value will cost you love, security, or belonging. For many people, money is not just a currency; it's an emotional battlefield. Saying no isn't just about guarding your time; it's about asserting your right to be fairly compensated, respected, and treated as more than a convenience.

This doesn't mean turning your life into a transaction or keeping score on every interaction. It means acknowledging that your labor, time, and expertise have value, and that when you give them away without boundaries, you're not being generous. You're being extracted.

And that extraction isn't always malicious. Sometimes it comes from friends or family who don't realize they're asking for too much. Sometimes it comes from clients or colleagues who assume your silence means consent. But the longer you allow the dynamic to persist, the harder it becomes to recalibrate it.

This is especially true for emotional labor, as support, listening, holding space, or managing dynamics in a group or relationship. This kind of labor is rarely acknowledged, let alone paid for. But for those who default to caretaker or mediator roles, it can become a full-time job with no paycheck and no time off. The financial cost isn't always obvious, but it's real. It's the opportunity cost of time you could've spent on your own growth, career, rest, or revenue-generating work.

And perhaps more dangerously, when your value becomes entangled with your ability to help for free, it starts to feel *wrong* to charge at all. You underquote. You offer extras. You apologize when you do ask for fair pay. All the while, your resentment builds, and your bank account doesn't.

To shift this, you must begin by questioning the stories you hold about worth. Who taught you that asking for more was greedy? Did that saying no to unpaid labor mean you were cold or unkind? That being generous meant being endlessly available, accessible, or affordable?

These aren't just economic beliefs; they're identity-level scripts. And the good news is, once you see them, you can start rewriting them.

You are not a bad person for charging fairly. You are not selfish for setting limits on your time. You are not unkind for declining something you once might have done for free. In fact, by doing so, you're modeling a different kind of integrity, one that values sustainability over sacrifice.

Reframing your relationship to money means getting honest about what your yes has cost you, not just in emotional bandwidth, but in literal hours you'll never get back, income you didn't earn, projects you postponed, and peace you sacrificed for the sake of being liked. That honesty may sting. But it also empowers you.

Because here's what happens when you start saying no to underpaid or unpaid commitments: you make room for more aligned, well-compensated, mutually respectful work. You begin to attract clients and collaborators who value boundaries instead of exploiting them. You start to teach people how to treat you, not with guilt or subtle pressure, but with clarity and respect.

This isn't theoretical. It plays out in real lives.

The entrepreneur who finally raised her rates after years of undercharging found that not only did her clients stay, but they also actually respected her more. The overcommitted employee who began saying no to weekend work found herself finally able to focus and perform better during the week, which led to a promotion she didn't even know was possible. The artist who stopped offering free designs for friends saw her portfolio deepen and her confidence return.

None of these outcomes came from hostility. They came from clarity. From a willingness to stop leaking value in the hope of earning approval.

When you protect your time and value, you don't become less generous. You become more intentional. More focused. And ironically, more impactful. Because a depleted giver ultimately benefits no one. A boundaried one can sustain their impact.

In the next segment, we'll bring this chapter full circle by looking at the ultimate cost of saying yes too often: the loss of your identity and direction. When other people's priorities shape your life, your purpose begins to blur, and reclaiming it requires more than just a few polite nos. It will require a reckoning.

When Saying Yes Erases Who You Are

One of the most haunting realizations a person can have is this: *I don't know who I am anymore,* not because of a single event or crisis, but because they've spent so long living in reaction to others, fitting into roles, fulfilling expectations, saying yes when they didn't want to, that they've lost track of their direction.

This is the most intimate cost of saying yes too often. It's not just the time, energy, or money you've surrendered. It's the slow erosion of your identity, worn down one small accommodation at a time.

When your default mode is agreement, your days are filled with what others want: their needs, their ideas, their pace. You become a chameleon, subtly adapting your preferences, personality, and priorities to match what the moment demands. You become the reliable one, the flexible one, the supportive one. And while those traits might win you affection, they slowly rob you of clarity. Your preferences grow hazy. You stop trusting your instincts. You lose the thread of your own life story.

It doesn't happen all at once. It happens gradually, invisibly. You stop pursuing specific goals, not because they were impossible, but because they were inconvenient to others. You stop speaking up, not because you have nothing to say, but because keeping the peace is easier. You stop dreaming, not because you lack imagination, but because you're too tired from managing everything else.

And then, one day, you realize your life looks nothing like you imagined it would. You've become a supporting character in your own story, managing scenes written by other people.

This is not drama. It's the quiet, daily reality for countless people who chronically overextend themselves. It's not that they lack ambition, creativity, or purpose; it's that those qualities have no room to breathe under the weight of all the yeses they've handed out. Their lives are dictated by momentum, not intention.

Saying no becomes more than a time-management strategy; it becomes a lifeline, a way to interrupt the drift and return to yourself. But to do that, you must be willing to acknowledge the extent of the drift. To name how you've abandoned your voice, your desires, your truth, not because you were weak, but because you were trained to believe that survival depended on it.

Many people who struggle with boundaries were never taught that they were allowed to have preferences, let alone assert them. They were raised in families or cultures where dissent was dangerous or disloyal. Where saying no meant risking connection, punishment, or shame. So, they learned early that the safest way to belong was to blend in. To please. To disappear.

Unlearning that requires more than scripts or time-blocking. It requires inner reprogramming. It requires reclaiming the parts of you that were deemed inconvenient, demanding, or selfish. It requires developing a relationship with your wants, many of which have gone dormant from disuse.

What do you enjoy? What do you desire when no one else is watching or asking? What would you choose if no one were influencing you?

These questions are disorienting at first. You may not have clear answers, and that's okay. The process of re-becoming yourself isn't about snapping back into place. It's about gently excavating the parts of you that have been buried under social expectation and emotional labor. It's about listening more closely to the voice inside you that says, *"This isn't right,"* or *"I want something else,"* and giving it space to speak louder.

This isn't selfishness. This is self-reclamation. It's not about rejecting connection; it's about building it on a foundation of truth.

Because when you don't know who you are, every relationship becomes a negotiation you're destined to lose. You show up as a half-version of yourself, always anticipating what others need, never standing fully in your truth. That kind of connection is brittle. It doesn't nourish you; it drains you. And the people in your life never get to meet the real you. Just the agreeable, adaptable, endlessly available mask.

Saying no is the first step toward taking that mask off.

It won't happen overnight. It may not feel comfortable. But it will feel *true*. And truth, over time, is what heals the split between who you are and who you've been pretending to be.

Sometimes the cost of constant yes isn't collapse, it's stagnation. You wake up to find that the vibrant, curious, creative self you once knew has faded into routine. You realize you've built a life around keeping others comfortable, but you're not at home in it. And that realization, while painful, is also powerful.

Because it means you're ready.

Ready to do the work of reconnecting with yourself. Prepared to stop performing and start choosing. Ready to ask better questions about your life. Ready to be known, not just liked.

This book isn't about creating boundaries so you can isolate yourself. It's about creating boundaries so you can participate in life more fully. So, you can write, speak, rest, connect, and create from a place of wholeness. So, you can stop scattering your energy and begin gathering it, cultivating it, and using it to build something that reflects your authentic self.

In the final segment of this chapter, we'll move from reflection to action. You'll be guided through a practical, personal audit that will help you examine what your chronic yes has cost you, and what you stand to gain by making a change.

An Honest Accounting of Your Yeses

There's a quiet but powerful moment that occurs when someone finally decides to take stock. To look back, not with shame or self-blame, but with clarity. It's the moment you sit down and say: *What has all this agreeing cost me?*

For many, this is a reckoning. A return to truth. Not the story you've been telling others, how you're just busy, or a helper, or "always on the go", but the deeper story underneath: the one about how you learned to function over, over give, and override your instincts.

This segment is about opening that ledger and beginning an honest accounting.

Start by thinking of the past month. Not a year, not a decade, just a month. Ask yourself: Where did my time go? Not just what you scheduled or recorded, but what you *spent*. How many hours went to meetings, favors, errands, check-ins, calls, and conversations that you didn't feel truly aligned with, but felt obligated to accept? How many mornings did you wake up tired, not from effort, but from emotional depletion?

If you're like most people reading this book, the answer may surprise you. We often normalize overextension so thoroughly that we don't realize we're operating at a deficit until we burn out, lash out, or shut down. But when you begin to look with new eyes, the pattern is hard to unsee.

Now shift your gaze to energy. When were you at your best? When did you feel resentful? What tasks gave you energy, and which ones drained it? What did you say yes to that led to regret, to resistance, to subtle or overt resentment?

This isn't about judgment. It's about honesty. And more than that, it's about pattern recognition.

When you start tracking where your energy leaks, you begin to see which yeses are costing you the most, not in one-off exhaustion, but in ongoing misalignment. The weekly call that leaves you emotionally flatlined. The standing meeting that adds nothing to your work but chews through your calendar. The friend who only calls when they need advice, not connection. The family expectation you fulfill while your own needs remain quietly unmet.

What emerges from this kind of audit isn't just data. It's grief.

Grief for how long you've tolerated discomfort for the sake of being liked. Grief for the ideas and goals you've put on the shelf because you were too busy fulfilling someone else's timeline. Grief for the version of yourself who needed to survive by saying yes, but who doesn't need to live that way anymore.

This grief is not only valid. It's necessary. Because in allowing yourself to feel it, you acknowledge what's been lost, and make space to decide what you will no longer give away so easily.

The cost of chronic compliance isn't abstract. It shows up in half-written books, unlaunched businesses, strained relationships, weakened immune systems, dreams deferred, and evenings spent numbing instead of living. It shows up in silence. In shallow breaths. In tight jaws and sleepless nights. In the quiet despair of someone who gave everything and doesn't know what's left.

But there's something else buried beneath that grief: resolve. The moment you acknowledge the cost, you begin to reclaim your agency. You start to realize that your time, your energy, your voice, and your direction are not just limited resources; they are sacred ones. They deserve protection not just from others, but from your unconscious patterns.

And that's the gift of the no. It's not a rejection of connection, ambition, or love. It's the boundary that allows those things to flourish without swallowing you whole.

Ask yourself now, with kindness and curiosity: What will I no longer say yes to?

Let the answers come not as a final list, but as an unfolding truth. You may not know everything right away. That's okay. What matters is that you begin to build the habit of asking. Before you agree, before you respond, before you default, *ask*. Is this mine to carry? Is this in alignment with who I am and where I'm going?

Because here's the most powerful truth of all: your yes is a contract. Every time you agree to something, you're entering into an energetic exchange. If you sign too many of those contracts without reading the fine print, you'll find yourself in a life composed of compromises you never consciously made.

You deserve better than that. And the people around you deserve the real you, not the worn-out version who's keeping everything afloat at her own expense.

This chapter was about cost. The next is about clarity.

We'll explore the difference between kindness and compliance, between genuine compassion and performative niceness. You'll learn how to stop confusing self-sacrifice with moral high ground, and how to begin living from a place of grounded, guilt-free integrity.

Because you don't have to betray yourself to belong, and you don't have to be a martyr to be meaningful.

Chapter 3: The Kindness Myth

For much of our lives, we are told to be nice. To share. To take turns. To help. To listen. To smile. These aren't bad lessons in themselves, but when delivered without nuance, they form a dangerous oversimplification: that the measure of a good person is how little space they take up.

As children, this message comes subtly at first. Don't interrupt. Be polite. Don't make a fuss. As we grow, the stakes increase. Be agreeable. Don't be selfish. Don't hurt anyone's feelings. Say yes when asked. Give others the benefit of the doubt. And above all: keep the peace.

Over time, we learn that our likability, especially for girls, people of color, or anyone raised in a caretaking role, is directly correlated to our compliance. We become fluent in reading the room, adjusting our tone, softening our needs, and shrinking our discomfort. We get good at being liked because we get good at being non-threatening.

This is the social contract of niceness: if you are accommodating enough, you will be safe. If you are selfless enough, you will be loved.

But what is lost in that exchange?

We rarely stop to ask what niceness is costing us. Because on the surface, it seems benign, even noble. Being nice gets praised. It makes others comfortable. It smooths conflict. It earns you compliments, promotions, second dates, and holiday invitations. It feels like a ticket into belonging. But scratch beneath the surface, and niceness reveals itself as something far more complicated.

Niceness is often a mask. A performance of warmth without authenticity. A pattern of behavior rooted not in care, but in fear, fear of rejection, of conflict, of being misunderstood. It's not always dishonest, but it is frequently incomplete. It tells only the part of the truth that won't make anyone uncomfortable.

Kindness, on the other hand, is something different. Kindness includes honesty. Kindness tells the truth with care, even when it's hard. Kindness has boundaries. Kindness says no when yes would be a lie. Kindness is not afraid to disappoint someone in the short term if it means honoring truth in the long term.

The difference is subtle but essential.

> ➢ Niceness is about smoothing things over. Kindness is about showing up with integrity.
> ➢ Niceness seeks approval. Kindness seeks alignment.
> ➢ Niceness avoids conflict at all costs. Kindness knows some conflict is necessary for growth.

When we confuse the two, we get stuck in a dangerous loop. We say yes when we mean no. We apologize for things that aren't ours. We minimize our needs to avoid "being a problem." We accommodate people who have not earned our energy. And then we wonder why we feel used, unseen, or vaguely resentful.

It's because we've mistaken emotional suppression for compassion.

Being "nice" often means hiding your truth. It means tucking away your discomfort so someone else doesn't have to feel theirs. It means carrying the emotional load of others at your own expense. But true kindness doesn't ask you to disappear. Genuine kindness makes space for others, yes, but also for yourself. If you've built your identity around being nice, this distinction can feel destabilizing. You may wonder, *if I stop being so accommodating, will people still love me? Will I still be good?* These are real fears, and they deserve compassion, not dismissal. You likely learned to be nice for very good reasons. It kept you connected. It made you safe. Maybe it protected you in a home where conflict wasn't allowed, and or earned you stability in a job or relationship where emotional expression was discouraged.

Niceness is often a trauma response dressed up as a virtue. But what kept you safe then may be keeping you stuck now. The version of you who learned to self-sacrifice for acceptance deserves gratitude, but she also deserves rest. She deserves the chance to learn a new way of relating to the world, one built not on compliance, but on clarity.

This chapter will guide you through that shift. We'll explore how people-pleasing gets mistaken for goodness, and how to begin reclaiming a definition of kindness that includes your needs, your limits, and your voice.

Because it's possible to be a deeply good person without constantly betraying yourself.

You can be compassionate and clear. You can be generous and discerning. You can care deeply about others without collapsing into them. But first, you must be willing to untangle the myth that being "nice" is the same as being kind.

In the next segment, we'll look more closely at the internalized roles many of us carry, the "good girl," the "reliable guy," the "peacemaker", and how these identities can trap us in cycles of over-giving. Because before you can rewrite the story, you need to see the script you've been living out.

The Good Girl, the Nice Guy, and Other Inherited Roles

You don't wake up one day and decide to become a people-pleaser. It doesn't happen with a single choice or moment. It happens slowly, over time, as you internalize the messages you're given about what it means to be "good."

You're praised for being easygoing, for sharing without being asked, for letting someone else go first. You learn that your emotional needs are secondary, or worse, that having them is a problem. You see how conflict makes the adults in the room tighten up, so you become the peacekeeper. You notice how much smoother life goes when you stay agreeable, predictable, and pleasant.

And before long, you're not just behaving this way, you're becoming it.

This is how the identity forms. For many women, it's the "good girl" script. Be sweet. Be polite. Be accommodating. Don't be loud. Don't be difficult. Don't be demanding. Good girls don't challenge. Good girls don't say no. Good girls don't make people uncomfortable.

For many men, it's the "nice guy" performance. Don't rock the boat. Be dependable. Be emotionally available, but not *too* emotional. Be strong but not too assertive. Say yes to what's asked of you, and maybe, just maybe, you'll be seen as good enough, worthy enough, needed sufficient.

There are other scripts, too: the responsible oldest child, the tireless caregiver, the selfless friend, the reliable employee, the emotional sponge. These roles differ in detail, but they all share one common theme: you learn to locate your goodness in how well you manage the needs of others.

These roles are sticky because they're rewarded. You're told you're mature for your age. Loyal. Thoughtful. Capable. But behind those compliments is a subtle bargain: *Keep being this way, and we'll keep loving you. Change the rules, and the approval goes away.*

The problem is, these scripts don't come with expiration dates. They don't loosen their grip as you grow older or more independent. They often tighten. By adulthood, you may not even realize that you're still performing. You think this is just who you are, reliable, supportive, helpful. And maybe you are all of those things. But if they've become so intertwined with your identity that you no longer know where your needs fit in, then they are no longer just personality traits. They are constraints.

What makes this particularly complicated is that these roles are often praised even as they deplete us. You're called "so strong" when you never ask for help. "So generous" when you cancel your plans to show up for someone else. "So easygoing" when you let someone else decide, again. What's missing from that praise is any recognition of what it costs you.

Because eventually, it does cost you, emotionally, physically, and spiritually. You become the container for everyone else's needs and feelings, but who's holding space for yours? Who sees you when you're not being helpful, or strong, or agreeable? Do you even know how to be seen in that way?

That's the danger of these roles. They're not just exhausting, they're invisibilizing. They keep you safe, but small. They offer connection, but it is conditional. And they shape your identity around utility instead of authenticity.

To begin shifting this, you must be willing to name the role you've taken on, not as an act of blame, but as a form of liberation.

Ask yourself: What identity do I perform to feel worthy? What part of me is always managing others' comfort? Who would I be if I weren't trying to be good?

These are not small questions. They're unsettling by design. They ask you to confront the possibility that your goodness has become a performance, and that your truth has been buried underneath it. They ask you to consider that being "good" isn't the same as being whole.

Many people are terrified to let go of their roles because they believe it's all that's keeping them connected. If I stop being the helper, who will still call? If I stop being agreeable, who will still invite me? If I stop fixing, who will still need me?

These are real fears, and yet, they point to a more profound truth. If your worth in a relationship depends on your self-abandonment, it's not a relationship. It's an arrangement.

You deserve more than arrangements.

You deserve a connection that doesn't require you to disappear. Love that doesn't hinge on compliance. Respect that doesn't demand silence.

But to get there, you must be willing to challenge the inner narrative that says being kind means being endlessly available, agreeable, or soft-spoken. It doesn't. Kindness can be fierce. Kindness can be boundary-laced. Kindness can say: *I love you, and I won't betray myself to make you more comfortable.* In the next segment, we'll dive deeper into what genuine kindness looks like when it includes honesty. Because the most loving thing you can sometimes do, for others and yourself, is to stop pretending and start telling the truth.

Honesty as an Act of Care

We are taught to associate kindness with comfort. But comfort and care are not always the same. Sometimes, the kindest thing you can do is to create discomfort, through honesty, through limits, through refusing to play along with a dynamic that is draining you or enabling someone else.

This is not how most of us were taught to define kindness. We were raised to believe that a kind person keeps the peace, says yes, and avoids friction. A kind person doesn't make things awkward. A kind person puts others first, even when it hurts. But there's a deeper kind of kindness, one that includes truth. And truth, by its very nature, sometimes causes discomfort.

Genuine kindness is not about protecting someone from every difficult feeling. Genuine kindness is saying, *I care about you enough to be honest,* even if it's messy, even if it's hard, even if it changes the nature of the relationship.

It takes courage to be honest when honesty risks rejection. But it also takes love, not just for the other person, but for yourself. It takes a belief that your truth is worthy of space, even if it causes disruption.

Too often, we equate kindness with approval. We think we're being nice by holding back what we think or need. But withheld truth creates distance. When you say yes but mean no, you're not giving someone your love; you're giving them a performance. When you agree outwardly but resent inwardly, the connection becomes hollow.

Genuine connection requires reality. And reality is sometimes uncomfortable.

If you've spent your life avoiding conflict, this can feel threatening. You may worry that honesty will push people away. And in some cases, it might. Not because you've been unkind, but because they were only attached to your compliance. But those who stay, those who grow with you through honesty, are the ones with whom real intimacy becomes possible.

Think of a moment when someone told you a hard truth with love. Maybe they told you they needed more space. Maybe they admitted they couldn't meet your expectations. Perhaps they said no to a request you thought they'd fulfill. If they delivered that truth with clarity and care, it may have hurt, but it also deepened your respect for them.

We crave this kind of clarity from others. And yet we withhold it from ourselves and the people we love. Not because we want to deceive, but because we don't want to cause harm. But here's the paradox: in avoiding harm, we often create a deeper one. We usually delay truth until it emerges sideways, through resentment, burnout, or emotional withdrawal.

This is why learning to say no kindly, clearly, and early is such an essential act of care. It prevents rupture later. It builds trust. It shows others and yourself that relationships can hold truth, not just performance.

This doesn't mean blurting your truth without tact or empathy. Honesty is not brutality. But neither is it silence. The work is in the middle path: truth delivered with care, boundaries delivered with clarity. No's delivered with enough respect that the person hearing them still feels seen, even if they don't get what they want.

This is a form of love we don't talk about enough. A kind of love that isn't built on sacrifice, but on structure. A love that says: *I value this connection enough to bring my whole self into it, even when that self has limits.*

When you begin to show up this way, something shifts in your relationships. Those who are accustomed to your automatic yes may feel surprised. Some may resist. But others will recognize your honesty as a kind of invitation: an opportunity to relate to the real you, not just the agreeable version of you.

Over time, you may find that your relationships become more honest, more resilient, and more mutual. You may also find that certain connections fall away, and while that can hurt, it's also clarifying. You begin to see who is truly capable of loving you as you are, not just as who you've been performing to be.

This process is not easy. It requires patience, especially with yourself. If you've built a lifetime on avoiding conflict, every honest no may feel like a small rebellion. And in a way, it is. It's a rebellion against the idea that being loved means being soft, silent, and self-sacrificing.

The truth is that the people you love deserve the real you. Not the polite version. Not the overextended one. Not the yes-woman or yes-man who smiles while their inner voice screams.

They deserve the version of you who tells the truth, even when it's hard. Who sets limits, even when it changes the dynamic? Who trusts that love can survive a no.

And you deserve that kind of love, too.

In the next segment, we'll explore how choosing kindness over niceness isn't always comfortable, but it is freeing. Because once you stop chasing comfort, you start building connection. Not just with others, but with your values, your integrity, and your power.

When Kindness Feels Like Conflict

When you begin living with more honesty, the world doesn't always applaud. The first reaction you often receive isn't admiration, it's discomfort. Maybe even pushback. People squint at you with suspicion: *You've changed. That's not like you. Are you okay?* What they mean is: *I was more comfortable when you were easier to manage.*

And this moment, when your truth first meets someone else's discomfort, is the critical one. It's where most people are tempted to retreat. To soften, to backpedal, to smooth it over. To convince others (and themselves) that they haven't changed, that they're still lovely, still agreeable, still easy to be around.

But what if being easy to be around is the highest goal?

What if your goal is no longer to be palatable, but to be whole?

The uncomfortable truth is this: when you shift from niceness to kindness, when you start telling the truth with integrity and setting boundaries with compassion, your relationships will feel the tremor. Niceness hides your needs. Kindness reveals them. Niceness avoids confrontation. Kindness walks through it, with care. Niceness maintains peace through suppression. Kindness maintains peace through clarity.

Most people have never experienced this kind of kindness. When you begin to embody it, they may misinterpret it. They may call it rude. They may call it selfish. They may even say you've lost your softness. But the softness they were used to was often compliance. What you're stepping into now isn't hardness, it's solidity.

There's a profound difference between being hard and being firm. Hardness is brittle, reactive, armored. Firmness is rooted, principled, and calm. The work of this chapter, and your new relationship with boundaries, is to stop hardening yourself against the world and instead root yourself in who you are.

Because niceness, at its core, is an avoidance strategy. It's how we avoid discomfort, confrontation, and risk. But the avoidance comes at a cost: it keeps you in relationships that require dishonesty. It keeps you at jobs that reward overextension. It keeps you locked in habits of self-erasure because the alternative, being misunderstood or disliked, is too frightening to face. Let's be honest: the moment you start being honest, some people will not like it.

That doesn't mean you've done something wrong. It means your role in their life is shifting. It means the quiet contract you both participated in, where you kept things smooth in exchange for affection or approval, is being renegotiated. And renegotiation is never without friction.

But friction isn't failure. It's movement. It's how you know you're no longer performing kindness but practicing it. Because genuine kindness doesn't avoid truth, it walks beside it. And absolute truth doesn't abandon kindness; it carries it, even when the weight is awkward.

You'll know you're stepping into this kind of living when your body starts to tell you the difference, when a yes no longer comes with tension, when a no feels clean, even if it's not received well. When your presence feels steady, even when others waver. You'll begin to experience what it's like to live from the inside out, instead of outside in.

This won't happen all at once. At first, your yeses might still come too quickly. Your no's might feel forced or shaky. You'll second-guess yourself. You'll wonder if you're being too rigid, too sharp, too selfish. That's normal. That's what transition feels like.

But each time you choose to say no when you mean no, or yes when it's truly aligned, you build trust with yourself. You show yourself that your internal compass is strong enough to guide you, even if others don't approve. You stop outsourcing your morality to others' reactions and instead begin to define your own.

This shift can feel lonely at times. But it's also liberating. Because once you're no longer chasing comfort at all costs, you can begin to chase what matters: connection, creativity, purpose, peace.

You realize that proper safety isn't in being liked, it's in being aligned.

And that's the quiet revolution. That's where real power begins. Not with shouting, defending, or justifying. But with standing. Calmly, kindly, and without apology. In your no. In your values. In your integrity.

In the next segment, we'll explore how to realign your values around compassion and boundaries, not as opposing forces, but as partners. You'll learn how to live a life where kindness isn't something you perform for others, but something you anchor within yourself.

Compassion Meets Boundaries

Many people believe, often unconsciously, that boundaries are cold and compassion is warm, and that choosing one excludes the other. We're conditioned to think that saying no is an act of withholding, of shutting down care, of closing ourselves off. And so we default to yes, to openness, to tolerance. But in doing so, we confuse compassion with collapse.

The truth is that boundaries are not the opposite of compassion; they are its foundation.

Without boundaries, compassion becomes unsustainable. It turns into martyrdom, into exhaustion masquerading as service. It becomes care given out of obligation rather than choice. And care without choice is not compassion, it's coercion. It's generosity drained of its essence.

To begin unlearning this, you need to look at your values. Not the values you were taught to perform, obedience, politeness, helpfulness, but the ones that resonate from your core. What do you stand for? What do you want to protect, not just in others, but in yourself?

Many of us have inherited a value system that prioritizes harmony over honesty, duty over desire, and appearance over truth. We're taught that to be compassionate means to be endlessly available, that to be moral means to be self-sacrificing, that to be strong means to carry everything without complaint.

But these aren't values. They're survival strategies dressed up as virtues.

Absolute values require thought. Choice. Discernment. They ask you to look at what you're genuinely trying to embody, not what others expect you to mirror. Ask yourself:

Do I value being kind or being liked? Do I value connection, or compliance? Do I value peace, or simply the absence of conflict? Do I value service, or do I fear being unnecessary?

These are not easy questions. They peel back the layers of identity you may have worn for decades. They confront you with the difference between what you've been praised for and what truly matters to you. But they are essential if you want to live a life where your boundaries are not a defense mechanism, but a declaration of your values.

To begin this process, you don't need to have every answer. What you need is a willingness to observe. Notice the moments when your yes feels heavy, when your kindness feels forced, when your care is laced with resentment. These are clues, not of your failure, but of your misalignment. They point you toward the boundary that wants to exist but hasn't yet been voiced.

Boundaries, when rooted in values, become an act of love. They say: I care enough to protect this relationship from my future resentment. I care enough about you and myself to keep things honest. I care enough not to perform.

In this way, boundary-setting becomes sacred work. It's not about control. It's not about domination. It's about staying connected without self-abandonment. It's about being in relationships where you don't have to lie, shrink, or pretend.

But this requires redefining kindness as something active, not passive. Not a reflex. Not a default. Kindness, when conscious, is a radical force. It can say: *I can't do this right now. I'm not available this weekend. I don't have the emotional bandwidth for this conversation today. That doesn't work for me. I need something different.*

These are not betrayals of kindness. They are expressions of it. Because they come from a place of truth, and truth is what makes kindness trustworthy.

So, as you continue on this path, begin crafting a new values map. Let go of the inherited scripts and start defining what compassion means to you, what it looks like, how it feels in your body, and how it aligns with your limits rather than erasing them.

You might discover that your version of kindness is quieter than what others expect. Or firmer. Or less available. That doesn't make it less accurate. It makes it more *yours*.

Because absolute values don't require universal agreement, they require congruence. When your values and your behavior align, something remarkable happens: your energy steadies. Your resentment fades. Your relationships shift from obligation to choice. Your presence becomes less fractured. You stop leaking energy into performances and start rooting it in truth.

And the more you live this way, the more you become a model for your friends, your children, and your coworkers, showing them what kind of bounded living can look like. You stop perpetuating the myth that kindness is synonymous with erasure. You show, through action, that kindness has a backbone. That boundaries are not barriers, they are bridges. They allow real connections to happen.

In the next and final segment of this chapter, we'll solidify this new way of seeing yourself, not as someone who must choose between kindness and boundaries, but as someone fully capable of both. You'll be guided through a reflective practice to begin living into your redefined values and cultivating compassion without self-sacrifice.

Living Kindness with Backbone

Now that you've begun to reexamine your values, to peel back the layers of people-pleasing and redefine what kindness truly means to you, it's time to step into practice, not perfectly, but intentionally.

This kind of shift doesn't happen overnight. You won't wake up tomorrow, suddenly immune to the urge to say yes out of guilt. You won't stop caring what people think. You won't eliminate all discomfort around boundaries. But what you *will* begin to develop is a new inner compass, one that points not to compliance, but to integrity.

And that compass will start to guide your choices in real time.

You might be about to reply "Sure!" to an invitation and pause, just long enough to check in with your body. You might feel the tug to smooth something over in a conversation and stop yourself, realizing you're about to lie by omission. You might hear someone vent for the third time this week and feel the familiar ache in your chest that says, *I can't keep holding this.*

These small moments are the proving ground for a new kind of kindness. Not the kind that requires your exhaustion, but the kind that reflects your values. This is what it means to live with a kind backbone. To speak from your center, rather than from your conditioning. To offer presence without performing. To express love without erasing yourself.

But to do that, you need to permit yourself, not just intellectually, but emotionally, to let go of the version of you that others found most convenient.

That version was never fake. It was adaptive. It kept you safe, liked, and included. It was born out of wisdom and survival. But if it no longer fits, fulfills, or no longer feels like truth, then it's time to thank it and let it evolve.

This next version of you, the one who says yes with clarity and no without guilt, will not be loved by everyone. But she will be trusted. Respected. Seen. And perhaps most importantly, she will begin to trust herself.

That trust grows every time you align action with your values, whether it's saying no because you mean it, saying yes with presence rather than pressure, or telling the truth, even if your voice shakes. When you rest, even if there's still something left on the to-do list. When you decline to carry someone else's emotions for them.

You are practicing not just boundaries, but self-trust.

And self-trust is the soil in which all meaningful growth is planted.

As we close this chapter, here is your invitation:

Begin living your redefined kindness, not as a posture, but as a path.

Speak kindly to others, yes. But speak kindly to yourself, too. Recognize when kindness means stepping forward, and when it means stepping back. Ask: *Is this kindness, or is this fear in disguise?* Ask: *Am I doing this from love, or from the belief that I must earn love by doing it?*

Let your body be your barometer. You don't have to think your way into integrity; you can feel your way there. Tight chest, shallow breath, creeping resentment, these are signs you're crossing into self-erasure. Lightness, clarity, energy, these are signs you're acting from truth.

Over time, this self-awareness becomes second nature. And the people around you will start to adjust. Some will fall away. Others will rise to meet you. But through it all, you'll be grounded. Not because you've hardened, but because you've rooted yourself in values that hold.

You can be kind without being small. You can be generous without being emptied. You can be loving without being agreeable. You can be honest and still be good.

Let this be your new definition of kindness: Truth spoken with care. Boundaries drawn with love. Compassion practiced without betrayal.

You don't have to choose between your integrity and your relationships. But if the choice arises, choose your integrity, so the relationships that remain are genuine.

In the next chapter, we'll move from philosophy to practicality. You'll learn exactly what boundaries are, how to recognize when they've been crossed, and how to begin defining and defending yours, not as a way of closing your heart, but as a way of honoring it.

Understanding that kindness and people-pleasing are not the same sets the stage for a crucial skill: boundary-setting. In the next chapter, we will build a clear foundation for what boundaries are, why they matter, and how they serve as the framework that supports authentic kindness and self-care.

Chapter 4: Drawing the Line

The Boundary You Never Learned to Name

Most people don't realize they have the right to set boundaries until after they have already been crossed. They often don't learn about boundaries from their parents, schools, or workplaces. Instead, they learn about boundaries from pain. From exhaustion. From that sharp internal pang that comes when you realize, too late, that something should've been a no.

You likely know the feeling. It arrives quietly, without fanfare. You say yes when your chest is tight. You stay on the call when you're mentally checked out. You answer the door even when everything in you wants solitude. These are not dramatic acts. They're subtle breaches, moments when your behavior disconnects from your inner truth.

You don't always know why you do it. Maybe you want to be kind. Perhaps you're afraid of disappointing someone. Maybe you've been conditioned to believe that your comfort should always be the last priority. Whatever the reason, the pattern is the same: you ignore the internal signal and comply with the external demand.

But over time, these minor violations add up. They wear you down. They build resentment where connection used to live. They turn kindness into currency, relationships into obligations, and your daily life into a series of commitments shaped by everything but your choosing.

This is what happens when you move through life without clear boundaries.

Not everyone starts boundary-less. But many people, especially those raised in high-demand environments, families with unpredictable emotions, institutions with rigid expectations, and cultures that prize obedience, are taught that boundaries are dangerous. That they signal rebellion. That they cause disruption. That they make it hard for you to love.

And so, to stay safe, to be good, to remain wanted, you soften. You become what the room needs. You respond instead of asserting. You blend instead of resisting.

The result? You learn to feel responsible for other people's comfort. For their perception of you. For their reactions to your limits. You believe, without quite realizing it, that it's your job to make everyone else feel okay, even if that means abandoning yourself.

This is where the boundary conversation must begin, not with how to say no, but with *why* it's been so hard to do so in the first place.

Because boundaries are not just practical, they are deeply emotional. They challenge your survival strategies. They confront the stories you've told yourself about what you must do to be safe, to be loved, to belong.

That's why learning about boundaries is not just a skill. It's a reclamation.

It's the act of stepping back into your center and saying: I get to choose what comes in and what stays out. I get to decide what I offer and what I withhold. I am not here to be endlessly available. I am not a resource for others to consume. I am a person with needs, limits, and sovereignty.

That shift, though decisive, is rarely easy. It means saying no when saying yes would be easier. It means being misunderstood. It means learning to tolerate the discomfort of standing your ground.

But it also means something else: it means coming home to yourself.

When you begin to establish boundaries, you start to feel your shape again. You begin to hear your preferences more clearly. You start to realize that you've been living according to other people's expectations rather than your values. You begin to distinguish between what's true and what's merely familiar.

This is why boundaries aren't selfish; they're clarifying.

They help you discern what's yours to carry and what's not. They help you show up more honestly in your relationships. They allow your yes to mean something. They restore dignity to your time and energy. And, perhaps most importantly, they offer a new path, one where you can be generous without being used, connected without being consumed, and present without being depleted.

But before that path can open, you have to recognize the signs of life without boundaries.

Think back to last week. How many conversations drained you, not because they were intense, but because they felt obligatory? How many "quick" tasks turned into half-hour diversions from your priorities? How many hours did you give away to things that didn't align with your goals, but felt like too much trouble to refuse?

This is what life without boundaries looks like: externally full, internally hollow. Always responsive, never rooted. Endlessly active, rarely aligned.

You don't have to live that way anymore.

What comes next in this chapter is a new language, a way to understand what boundaries are, how to feel them in your body, how to name them without shame, and how to begin using them not to create distance, but to create *clarity*.

Because clarity is what people crave, not just from you, but around you, and when you begin to live with clarity, everything changes. You stop reacting to life and start shaping it. You stop defaulting to "yes" and start responding with intention.

And it all begins here: with the quiet decision that your life, your energy, your time, and your peace are not accidental; they are sacred.

In the next segment, we'll explore the anatomy of a boundary, what it is, how it functions, and why it's not a wall but a doorway. We'll begin giving form to something you've always needed but maybe never had permission to claim.

What a Boundary Is

It's easy to think of boundaries as brick walls, rigid structures that separate us from others, keeping things out, keeping people at a distance. But real boundaries are not about building barriers. They are about creating clarity. They don't exist to cut you off from connection. They exist to make connections safer, more honest, and more sustainable.

A boundary is, at its simplest, a clear statement of what is okay and what is not OK for you.

That's it. It's not a judgment of someone else. It's not a punishment. It's not even a negotiation. It's simply a personal truth expressed in a way that defines your emotional, physical, or energetic limits.

If you grew up thinking of boundaries as confrontational or mean, this definition may feel too simple. But boundaries, when understood correctly, are acts of maturity and respect. They let people know what version of you they're going to get. They remove the guesswork. They set the stage for clearer expectations and less resentment on both sides.

Most people don't realize that boundaries exist, whether you name them or not. You already have internal lines, lines that get crossed when someone speaks to you with disrespect, when someone monopolizes your time, when someone touches you without consent, or when you're asked to do something that feels misaligned. You think the boundary in your body long before you name it with your mouth.

But if you don't name it, the boundary gets crossed again and again. Not because others are malicious, but because you haven't told them where the line is.

Think of a boundary like a property line. If you don't mark it, people will walk across it, sometimes unintentionally. But once you post a sign, once you say, "This is where my space begins," everything changes. The line is not a weapon. It's not an accusation. It's a declaration: *this is where I live.*

The same is true for emotional boundaries. When you say, "I'm not available to talk about that right now," or "I need twenty-four hours to respond to this," or "That's not a topic I'm comfortable discussing," you are not closing the door on connection. You are creating the conditions in which you can connect without self-sacrificing.

And here's the irony: when you create those conditions, people trust you more. Because you're not unpredictable. You're not agreeable one day and resentful the next. You're not silently accumulating frustration that spills out in unspoken ways. You are clear. You are anchored. You are honest.

Boundaries can take many forms, depending on what you're protecting. There are physical boundaries (who can touch you and how), time boundaries (when you're available and for how long), emotional boundaries (what topics you'll engage with, how much you're willing to hold), energetic boundaries (how much presence and attention you can offer), and even digital boundaries (who can contact you, how quickly you'll respond, what kind of content you're willing to consume).

These aren't selfish, they're strategic. They protect the resources you need to show up in your life with intention, vitality, and peace.

Without them, everything leaks. Your calendar becomes filled with other people's priorities. Your inbox fills with demands. Your energy is scattered between too many conversations, too many responsibilities, and too much exposure. And when you try to regroup, when you cancel or withdraw, you often feel guilt or shame for needing space you should've claimed in the first place.

That's why boundaries must begin with internal honesty. You can't set boundaries with others until you're clear with yourself.

You have to be willing to admit what you want, what you can give, and what you can no longer tolerate.

That clarity is the seed. The boundary grows from there.

But here's where most people struggle: they wait until they're overwhelmed before they set a boundary. By then, it's not a calm statement; it's a crisis. They've said yes too many times. They've stayed silent too long. They've carried what wasn't theirs until their body, their emotions, or their relationships start to break under the pressure.

And when the boundary finally comes out, it doesn't land as a healthy limit; it lands as a shutdown, a shutdown that shocks others because any earlier signal didn't precede it.

This is why preventative boundaries are so powerful. When you set them early, from a place of self-awareness, not anger, not burnout, you reduce the need for future damage control. You build a foundation of respect and predictability in your relationships. You signal to others that you are not a limitless resource. You are a person, a person with shape, rhythm, limits, and needs.

It's worth repeating that boundaries are not walls. They are structures of safety. They are not about exclusion. They are about invitation, an invitation to meet you where you are, not where you're pretending to be.

They are also not static. Boundaries can change. What you could once give freely may now feel draining. What you used to tolerate may now feel intolerable. This doesn't mean you're becoming selfish. It means you're evolving. And as you grow, your boundaries must evolve too.

In the next segment, we'll explore how to identify when a boundary has been crossed, sometimes in obvious ways, but more often in subtle ones. Before you can speak your boundaries out loud, you need to sharpen your awareness of how your body and emotions signal that something is off.

Feeling the Breach Before You Can Name It

Before a boundary is broken in the world, it is broken in the body.

You feel it before you can articulate it. A sudden heaviness in your chest. A tightening in your throat. A prickle behind your eyes. A drop in your stomach that feels like sinking or nausea. Your hands might clench. Your heart might race. Your breath shortens. You override it quickly, because you've been taught to, but your body knows. Your body always knows.

One of the most powerful things you can do in the journey of reclaiming your boundaries is to learn how to listen to these signals without brushing them aside. They are not irrational. They are not inconvenient. They are not evidence of being "too sensitive." They are data. Emotional and physiological indicators that something in the interaction is not sitting right with you, even if the moment seems benign from the outside.

Not all boundary breaches are apparent. Sometimes they show up as someone speaking over you, again and again, until your voice disappears. Sometimes it's a friend unloading every personal crisis onto you, never asking if you have space to hold it. It could be a colleague who sends last-minute work late into the night, assuming you'll catch it. Or a partner who jokes about

74

something you've asked them not to, insisting you're just being dramatic when you ask them to stop.

These are not always explosive offenses. But they are boundary violations. Not because the actions are always cruel, but because they ignore, dismiss, or override your limits.

And when those boundaries are consistently ignored, even in subtle ways, you begin to learn that your discomfort is negotiable. That your needs are flexible. Your space isn't truly *yours* unless someone else agrees it should be.

The danger of these minor, consistent violations is that they're often rationalized. You tell yourself it's not a big deal. You tell yourself they didn't mean to. You tell yourself you're overreacting. And in doing so, you internalize the breach. You make it your job to tolerate the harm, rather than their job to stop causing it.

This is what boundary confusion looks like: when you feel hurt but can't explain why. When your yes feels loaded, but you give it anyway. When you say "it's fine," but your gut twists with every word.

Learning to recognize boundary breaches starts with unlearning the reflex to self-dismiss. It means taking your feelings seriously, even when they seem inconvenient. It means getting curious instead of critical when your body says *no* before your mind catches up.

Here's the truth: your discomfort is meaningful. It's not proof you're broken. It's proof you're alive and aware.

Discomfort is not always a sign that something is wrong with you. It can be a sign that something is wrong with the dynamic, and that you've grown too used to ignoring it.

To begin decoding your internal signals, start by observing your body in everyday scenarios. What happens when someone texts you at midnight expecting an answer? What do you feel when a family member makes a demand masked as a favor? What shifts in your body when someone talks *at* you for an hour without asking a single question in return?

These moments matter. Because while the world often celebrates boundary-breakers as "go-getters," "bold personalities," or "just direct," those who they impact usually walk away feeling flattened, diminished, or used.

You don't have to wait until you can perfectly articulate your needs to begin honoring them. You can start by noticing the flinch. The pullback. The inner resistance. That's the first sign of a boundary trying to rise. It might not yet have a language. But it's real.

Once you start naming these breaches, especially the small ones, you begin reclaiming the space to respond differently. You can say: "Actually, I'd like to finish my thought." You can say: "I don't have the bandwidth for this conversation right now; can we revisit it later?" You can say: "That joke doesn't land well with me, let's not go there." And you can tell it without apology.

But you can't speak boundaries that you don't yet feel. That's why this segment is about attunement, about relearning how to trust your signals instead of overriding them for the sake of being pleasant.

Some boundary breaches are cumulative. One conversation, one comment, one ask may not feel like a crisis, but over time, the repetition chips away at your sense of agency. It teaches you to remain silent to maintain peace. And peace built on silence is not peace, it's suppression.

This is where people often start to feel burned out in their relationships, work, and self-worth. Because they are expending energy holding in what they need to be letting out. They are managing others' emotions while neglecting their own.

And what's often beneath that behavior is a fear that if they do name their boundary, the connection will break. That the relationship won't survive the assertion of their needs. And sometimes, that fear is valid. Sometimes, it's happened before.

But the question is not whether everyone will accept my boundaries. The question is, do I want to build my life around people who only value me when I have none?

If the answer is no, then you must begin listening to your body, listening to your gut, and listening to the parts of you that are tired of shrinking.

In the next segment, we'll look at the most common myths about boundaries, the lies that keep you afraid to set them, and the truths that can liberate you. Because once you stop believing that boundaries are rude, selfish, or unkind, you can begin practicing them with clarity, confidence, and peace.

Myths That Mute You

Before you can live a boundaried life, you have to face down the beliefs that keep you from even considering it. For many, these aren't just thoughts; they're inherited mantras, internalized rules. Scripts passed down from families, cultures, religions, and workplaces that tell you what you're allowed to want, need, and say.

And more often than not, these rules are designed to preserve harmony, not health. Obedience, not truth. Appearances, not authenticity.

The first myth sounds innocent enough: **"Boundaries are selfish."**

This belief is one of the most deeply ingrained, especially for those raised to prioritize others' needs above their own. The logic goes something like this: If you loved people, you wouldn't limit them. If you were generous, you'd always be available. If you were strong, you wouldn't need to say no.

But real love does not require self-erasure. Real generosity is not measured by how much of yourself you give away. True strength is knowing where your edge is and honoring it. Boundaries are not selfish. They are what allow your care to have structure. Without boundaries, your giving becomes unsustainable. You help with depletion. You listen with resentment. You stay, but only in body, not in spirit.

The second myth? "Boundaries are mean or rude."

This myth survives because we've equated directness with hostility. Especially in cultures or families where politeness was prioritized over truth, the idea of saying "no" or "I need something different" is interpreted as an attack. But here's the truth: there is nothing rude about stating your limit with calm clarity. Boundaries do not require cruelty. They do not need drama. They can be delivered with compassion, kindness, and softness, yet still be firm.

Think of someone you trust deeply. Chances are, that trust didn't come from their endless compliance. It came from their consistency. Their clarity. Their honesty. That's what boundaries create. Not distance, but dependability.

Another pervasive belief is "If I set a boundary, people will leave."

This one runs deep, especially for those who have experienced abandonment, rejection, or emotional volatility in the past. When you've learned that love is conditional, tied to your ability to please or perform, the idea of asserting a need feels like inviting abandonment.

And yes, sometimes people will resist your boundaries. Sometimes they will push back. But those who walk away when you express your limits are not rejecting you. They are revealing that their attachment to you was based on access, not respect. That their comfort came from your silence, not your wholeness.

You are not responsible for how others respond to your boundaries. You are responsible for setting them, compassionately and consistently. The rest is not yours to carry.

Another sticky myth is "Once I set a boundary, it should be respected right away."

We'd all love for boundaries to be received with a nod and a thank you. But real life is messier. People don't constantly adjust right away. Sometimes they misunderstand. Sometimes they test the limits. Sometimes they're so used to your previous patterns that they think your "no" is temporary or negotiable.

That doesn't mean your boundary isn't valid. It means you're disrupting a dynamic, and like any disruption, it takes time to settle. The work is not just in *setting* the boundary, but in *reinforcing* it when it's challenged. That's where your power gets tested and strengthened.

And then there's the hidden myth: "If I were confident, I wouldn't need boundaries."

This idea often lurks beneath perfectionism and over-functioning. If I were stronger, I wouldn't get overwhelmed. If I were more competent, I wouldn't feel drained. If I were healed, I wouldn't need to push back.

But boundaries are not evidence of weakness. They are evidence of *self-awareness*. They don't mean you're fragile. They mean you're wise. Every time you name a boundary, you're not failing; you're leading.

Some of the most grounded, confident people you know likely have firm boundaries in place. You don't notice them because they've normalized them so well. They don't make a show of it. They don't argue. They don't overexplain. They don't overextend.

This is the clarity boundaries offer: not grand gestures, but grounded rhythms. Not drama, but steadiness.

When you release these myths, you begin to open up space for a different way of living. A way in which your needs are not a nuisance, your voice is not a threat, and your no is not a betrayal.

Instead, your needs become instructions for others on how to care for you. Your voice becomes a signal of safety. Your no becomes a way of preserving, not punishing, the connection.

As you continue reading, notice which of these myths you've carried. Not with judgment, but with curiosity. Ask: *Where did I learn this? Who benefits when I believe it? What becomes possible when I let it go?*

SAGE MONROE

These questions are not just theoretical; they're transformative. They give you permission to stop fighting your boundaries and start practicing them, not as apologies, but as affirmations of your worth.

In the next segment, we'll move from beliefs to embodiment. You'll learn how to visualize your life with boundaries in place, not as a fantasy, but as a map. A way to see, feel, and begin shaping the life that becomes possible when your limits are honored.

The Life You Draw

Before boundaries can become habits, they must become real. Not just as concepts you understand, but as experiences you can *feel*. This is why boundary work must eventually move from the head to the body, from theory to image, from abstract permission to lived reality.

One of the most effective ways to begin this shift is through visualization. Not wishful thinking, but intentional imagining. Seeing your life as it is, then seeing the version of it that exists when your needs are named, your time is protected, and your energy is respected. Seeing the contrast gives shape to your intention. It makes the invisible real.

Let's begin.

Close your eyes if you're somewhere you can. Take a slow, deliberate breath. And picture your current life as a room. Please don't force it. Let it form in your mind. It might look like your actual home, or something more symbolic, such as a cluttered

81

office, a house with no walls, or a shared space where you're unsure what belongs to you and what belongs to others.

Notice the door. Is it open, cracked, or wide? Do people walk in without knocking? Do they stay too long? Do they bring messes they expect you to clean up?

Now, picture your calendar. Do you see blocks of open time? Or is it overfilled, double-booked, scribbled with obligations? Is there space to breathe, to rest, to do nothing without guilt?

Now scan the room for your emotions. Where are they? Are they buried under piles of other people's needs? Are they pushed into the corner because there's no room left? Do you even see them at all?

What you're picturing now is a life without boundaries. One where you exist, but only in response to everything around you. One where others define your shape. One where clarity is missing, and everything feels urgent, exposed, and heavy.

Now, gently, change the picture.

Inhale. Exhale.

Begin building the room again, this time with boundaries.

This new room has a sturdy front door. There's a bell, a lock. You choose who enters, and when. You can say no without yelling. You can say yes without hesitation. There is a schedule on the wall that honors your priorities. It includes time to create, to move, to rest. There are private areas inside this room that are only accessible to those who are invited.

You see yourself standing inside. Upright. Present. You are not defensive, you are calm. Not on edge, you are grounded. The people who are here respect the space because you have taught them how.

Your emotions are visible now, resting, moving, and expressing. You are not carrying more than your share. You are not responsible for fixing or holding everything. You are not a resource for endless giving. You are a human being with shape, rhythm, and breath.

This is not an impossible dream. It is the visual representation of a boundaried life.

For many people, doing this exercise often results in an emotional response. Some feel sadness. Others feel relief. Some feel grief for the time spent living in rooms without walls, or in spaces built entirely for others. Some feel afraid, because this new room, while peaceful, also feels unfamiliar. Foreign.

But if that version of life feels foreign, it's not because it's wrong; it's because it's new.

And newness requires time, repetition, and practice to become embodied.

That's why this visualization isn't a one-time event. It's a tool. Something you can return to when you start to slip. When you say yes out of reflex. When you override your discomfort. When you forget that you're allowed to protect your peace without apology.

Each time you visualize your boundaried life, you strengthen the neural and emotional pathways that make it real. You begin to shift your inner blueprint. You show yourself what it looks like, what it feels like, and why it matters.

Because here's the truth: until you know what you're moving toward, it's hard to leave behind what you're stuck in.

The unbounded life is full of reaction. The boundaried life is full of choice. The unboundaried life feels chaotic and draining. The boundaried life feels intentional, even if it's not always easy.

But perhaps most importantly, the boundaried life is not a rejection of others. It's an affirmation of yourself. It's not about isolation, it's about sovereignty. It's about building a life where you are not just performing or surviving, but living, fully and freely.

In the final segment of this chapter, we'll begin integrating all we've covered. You'll receive anchoring practices and questions to help you start designing and defending your boundaries, not just in your mind, but in your everyday life.

From Insight to Action, Living the Boundaried Life

By now, you've begun to see the contours of a life shaped by clarity instead of compliance. You've seen that boundaries are not rejection, but protection. Not cruelty, but care. Not a defense against love, but a framework that allows real love, honest connection, and sustainable energy to exist.

Still, knowing what boundaries are is different than living them. Insight doesn't create change. Action does. Embodiment does. Repetition does. And like anything worth learning, boundaries are a practice. Not something you perfect, but something you recommit to over and over again.

It begins in small moments. Saying, "I'll need to think about that before I agree," instead of defaulting to a quick yes and holding your silence when you feel the urge to over-explain.

Choosing not to answer a text the moment it arrives and allowing someone to be disappointed without rushing in to fix it.

These moments matter. They're not minor. They are the new muscles you're building, flexing your capacity to tolerate the discomfort that once made you abandon yourself. And like physical muscles, they grow through consistency, not force.

Don't wait for the perfect time. Don't wait until you feel entirely confident. Begin now, where you are, with what you have.

Perhaps your first step is to identify one area of your life where you feel most overextended. Maybe it's work, where other people's urgencies constantly hijack your schedule. Maybe it's a friendship that leans heavily in one direction. Perhaps it's your internal relationship with rest, the guilt you feel when you stop moving. Wherever the pressure is greatest, that's usually where a boundary is most needed.

Boundaries are easiest to build when they are specific. Not abstract declarations like "I need more space" or "I need to stop being so nice," but tangible shifts in how you show up and what you allow. For example: "I won't respond to work emails after 7 PM." "I will not engage in conversations where I feel emotionally dumped on without consent." "I will say no to social plans that I agree to out of guilt rather than desire."

These are not just decisions. They are statements of self-respect.

Of course, setting boundaries will not always feel smooth. Sometimes your voice will shake. Sometimes you'll feel like a fraud. Sometimes, you'll over-correct, setting boundaries too harshly or too suddenly because you're trying to undo years of silence in one conversation.

That's okay. Clumsiness is part of learning. It means you're doing the work. It means you're trying something new. And you're allowed to be both powerful and imperfect at the same time.

What matters is that you notice when you abandon yourself and choose to return.

The return is the practice.

You may need to return every day. To your needs. To your values. To the version of yourself that isn't always convenient for others but is deeply aligned with who you're becoming.

Let that version of you take up more space.

Let her say no without apology.

Let her disappoint others when necessary, not out of malice, but out of clarity.

Let her speak without shrinking, rest without guilt, and leave when she needs to.

This is the boundaried life. Not one without connection, but one where connection doesn't require performance. Not one without service, but one where service flows from overflow, not depletion.

To help you integrate this further, consider asking yourself these three anchoring questions at the end of each day:

> ➤ Where did I override my own needs today?
> ➤ Where did I honor my boundaries, even if it was uncomfortable?
> ➤ What would it look like to move one step closer to clarity tomorrow?

These are not tests. They are invitations—touchpoints to help you notice your growth, however subtle, however slow.

Because this isn't about becoming someone new, it's about finally becoming yourself.

In the chapters ahead, we'll move into more applied territory. We'll explore the inner resistance you may still feel when saying no. The guilt. The fear. The anxiety. We'll work with those emotional blocks, not as obstacles to bulldoze, but as signals, messages from an inner system that's trying to protect you, even if it's using outdated methods.

For now, breathe.

You've done more than read a chapter. You've taken back something that many people never even realize they lost: your right to define your limits.

Your life gets to have shape. Your time gets to have edges. Your energy gets to have direction.

And your boundaries, when spoken with truth and anchored in love, are not something to hide or explain away.

They are something to stand on.

Chapter 5: When Saying No Feels Wrong

Understanding the Emotional Block

You've made the decision. You know you're allowed to have boundaries. You've imagined what life could look like when you stop giving from depletion. You've even tried to say no once or twice, and still, the guilt hits you like a wave.

It's a familiar, almost reflexive sensation. The moment you say no, especially to someone who's used to hearing yes, something in your chest tightens. You feel a prickle of shame, like you've just done something wrong. You second-guess your decision. You wonder if you were too harsh, too abrupt, too selfish. And the part of you that was beginning to find its voice goes quiet again.

This is the hidden barrier to boundaries: not that we don't know how to say no, but that it *feels bad* when we do.

Not just awkward. Not just unfamiliar. Bad, morally, emotionally, and sometimes even physically.

This is what keeps most people stuck in patterns of compliance. Not a lack of information or willpower, but the unresolved emotions that flood the body in the aftermath of asserting oneself. The guilt, the fear, the shame. These aren't just feelings; they're coded messages. And they were planted early.

Many of us were taught, long before we had language for it, that saying no comes with consequences. Maybe you were punished for disobedience. Perhaps you were praised for being "easy," "low maintenance," or "so helpful." Maybe love was conditional, offered when you pleased others, withheld when you had needs of your own.

In environments like these, guilt becomes a built-in response to self-expression. It doesn't mean your boundary is wrong. It means your nervous system has been trained to associate boundary-setting with danger.

This is crucial to understand. Because if you don't realize what's happening, you'll think the guilt is a sign to back down. You'll think it's a signal that you've done something bad. But guilt is not always a compass pointing to wrongdoing. Sometimes, it's just a reflex from a story that no longer fits your life.

This chapter is about learning to decode that guilt. To see it not as a stop sign, but as a doorway. A signpost that says: *You're stepping into new territory. This discomfort is growing on you.*

You may also feel fear, not just of confrontation, but of disconnection. The fear that saying no will create distance. That someone will be hurt. That someone will walk away. And sometimes, yes, that will happen. But the pain of that loss is often less damaging than the quiet, chronic pain of self-abandonment.

Fear is loud at first, especially when you're disrupting long-held patterns. Your body reads it as risk. And in a way, it is a risk, a risk to your old identity, to the version of you who kept everything together by staying silent.

But that version of you was never meant to last forever. It was meant to get you here. And now you're ready for something more honest, more expansive, more whole.

There's also shame. Shame is different from guilt. Guilt says, "I did something wrong." Shame says, "I *am* wrong." When you say no and feel shame, it's often because a deeper story has been triggered. A belief that your needs are too much. That your presence is a burden. That if you take up space, you'll lose love. Shame is a powerful silencer. It makes you doubt your right to exist on your terms. But it's also a story. A learned story. And like all stories, it can be rewritten.

To do that, you need tools that go deeper than language. You need practices that work with your body, not just your thoughts. Because boundary-setting is not just an intellectual act, it's a nervous system event. It happens in your breath, your muscles, your gut. That's why even small acts of assertiveness can trigger big waves of emotion.

But you don't have to push those feelings away. You don't have to pretend they're not there. The work is to *stay with them*. To sit inside the discomfort without making it mean something is wrong. To tell yourself: *I'm allowed to feel guilty and still honor my no.*

This is how reprogramming begins.

It's not clean, easy, or instantaneous. But it's powerful. Because each time you say no and survive the guilt, each time you hold your boundary and breathe through the shame, you teach your body a new lesson: *I can do this. I can say no and still be safe. Still be loved. Still be okay.*

And slowly, the guilt quiets. The fear softens. The shame begins to dissolve.

In the next segment, we'll explore where these emotional blocks come from in more depth, tracing them back to the internalized rules and "should" statements that have quietly governed your behavior for years. You'll learn to identify the specific stories driving your discomfort so that you can begin replacing them with truths rooted in self-respect.

Dismantling the "Should", Where Guilt Begins

Long before we say our first adult yes, we've already learned hundreds of ways to override our instincts. We're taught to obey, to share, to be helpful, to be quiet, and to be polite. We're trained to please long before we're taught to protect ourselves. And we carry these lessons forward, not as conscious choices, but as internal scripts.

These scripts often sound like a quiet, relentless voice in your head: You should help. You should go. You should say yes and deal with it later. You should be more understanding. You should be grateful they even asked you. You shouldn't make it a big deal.

This voice is not your enemy. It's an echo. A repetition of everything you were taught about what makes you good, lovable, practical, and safe.

These "shoulds" don't always come from cruel places. Sometimes they come from parents who wanted you to be well-mannered. From teachers who rewarded obedience. From cultures that equate respect with silence. From faith traditions that elevate sacrifice above self-awareness. From peer groups that value conformity over truth.

The messages weren't always malicious. But they were loud. And repetition is powerful. Eventually, these "shoulds" become internal law.

You don't question whether you want to help; you assume you're supposed to. You don't pause to feel your no, you override it out of habit. You don't ask if it's fair, you act before you think.

And when you do try to resist, when you say no or pause or ask for space, the backlash doesn't even have to come from others. It comes from within. A pang of guilt. A flicker of shame. A whisper that says, *You're disappointing someone.*

This is why unlearning "should" is foundational to boundary work.

Because "should" is not the voice of your intuition, it's the voice of your programming.

It doesn't ask what you want. It tells you what you owe. It doesn't consider your capacity. It tells you your role. And the more you obey it, the more you forget to ask the most important question of all: *What do I need right now?*

Learning to hear your voice underneath the "shoulds" takes time. The scripts are sticky. They've become so normal that you don't notice them. They hide in words like "just," "only," and "have to." They show up when you're about to opt out of a plan but suddenly feel obligated, when you're about to speak up but remember how hard that conversation will be. When you want to rest but can't shake the feeling that you're being lazy.

This is the inner resistance we're up against, not ignorance, but conditioning.

And here's the tricky part: sometimes the "should" even wears the costume of kindness. You should be there for them; they need you. You should make the effort; it's the right thing to do. You should say yes, it's not that big a deal. But kindness that requires you to betray yourself isn't kindness. It's a compulsion.

There's a difference between generosity and guilt-driven compliance. There's a difference between care and control. And the way to begin separating them is to catch the "should" in real time.

When it arises, pause.

Instead of following it automatically, ask: Who says I should? What would happen if I didn't? Is this aligned with my values, or just my fear?

These questions don't always produce immediate clarity. Sometimes they bring discomfort. That's okay. The goal is not to rush to a different answer, but to create enough space for an *honest* one.

Sometimes you'll still choose to say yes. But it will come from the agency, not obligation. And that difference matters.

Because a yes without freedom is not a yes, it's a performance.

As you continue to dismantle these internal rules, you'll start to notice where they came from. Maybe your family never talked about boundaries. Perhaps saying no was seen as a form of defiance. Maybe the only way you felt valued was when you were needed. Possibly, you were praised for being mature, not because you were ready, but because you had no other option.

And once you see the roots, you begin to reclaim the soil.

You begin to realize that the guilt you feel is not proof that you're wrong. It's a residue. A reflex. A result of living in a world where your compliance was praised louder than your clarity.

Let that awareness be your turning point, not into rebellion, but into reclamation.

In the next segment, we'll explore how to work with these emotional responses in your body, not to eliminate them, but to understand and soothe them, so you can build a relationship with guilt and fear that doesn't sabotage your boundaries.

Because the goal isn't to *never* feel guilt, it's to know what to do when it arrives.

Soothing the System, Your Body's Role in Saying No

When you say no, especially if you're not used to it, your body often doesn't feel relief right away. It feels alarmed. Even if your words are steady, your heart might pound. Your chest might tighten. You may feel nauseous, lightheaded, or shaky. You might second-guess yourself immediately, wondering if the discomfort means you've made a mistake.

But it's not a mistake. It's your nervous system doing what it was designed to do: respond to perceived threat.

For most people, especially those raised in environments where boundaries weren't modeled or allowed, saying no triggers a survival-level response. The moment you assert yourself, your body senses disruption. And disruption, particularly of relational harmony, can feel dangerous if your safety was once dependent on being agreeable, accommodating, and emotionally predictable.

This is not irrational. It's adaptive. It's how your body learned to keep you safe.

And that's why intellectual insight isn't enough. You can understand, on a mental level, that you're allowed to say no, but if your body is still registering that no as unsafe, you'll either avoid it or say it and then collapse under guilt.

This is where the nervous system's work becomes essential. Because boundary-setting isn't just a communication skill, it's a somatic one. It involves your breath. Your posture. Your muscle tension. Your ability to stay present inside discomfort without panicking or dissociating.

The first step is awareness. Begin to notice what your body does before, during, and after you say no. Do you brace? Do you fidget? Does your voice get tight, your shoulders rise, your jaw clench? Do you immediately try to justify your decision, to soften the boundary, or apologize for it?

These are cues, not of failure, but of a body that is used to managing threats by keeping others happy.

So, what do you do when your body protests your boundary, even when you know it's right?

You soothe. You co-regulate. You create internal safety so that your boundary doesn't have to rely on someone else's approval.

Here are three simple, repeatable practices that help:

1. When we're in a stress response, our breathing becomes shallow and fast. To signal safety, lengthen your exhales. Place a hand on your belly and another on your chest, and guide your breath downward. Let your belly expand, not your chest. Count four in, hold for two, exhale for six. Repeat a few rounds. This resets your baseline and tells your system: you're safe.. Feel your feet on the floor. Press your hands into a surface, your thighs, a chair arm, or a table. Use sensation to bring you back to the present.

When your thoughts spiral ("They'll be mad," "I shouldn't have said that," "What if they leave?"), Sensation grounds you in the here and now. And in the here and now, you're okay.

2. Out loud or silently, affirm what's true: It's okay to have needs. I'm allowed to say no. My safety doesn't depend on being agreeable. This feels hard because it's new, not because it's wrong. Self-talk matters. Especially in the fragile moments after a new behavior, when your system is seeking feedback. Be the feedback. Speak to yourself as a wise protector, not a critical voice.

You don't need to be fearless to hold a boundary. You need to be willing to feel the fear and not let it drive the decision.

Over time, with repetition, your body begins to recalibrate. It stops interpreting assertiveness as danger. It learns that discomfort is survivable. The idea that saying no doesn't mean you'll be abandoned or attacked, and that you can feel fear and still follow through.

This is nervous system reprogramming. And it's one of the most essential pieces of boundary work, because if you don't include your body, you will always be fighting it. You'll get stuck in a loop: understand the boundary, set the boundary, feel guilt, collapse, overexplain, and return to over-giving.

But if you work *with* your body instead of against it, you create a different loop: notice the impulse, breathe through the tension, hold the line, feel the fear, soothe it, and repeat. Each time gets easier. Each time, your body builds evidence that you're not in danger when you honor your truth.

This is slow, powerful work.

It won't always feel clean. Some days, you'll regress. You'll cave when you wanted to hold firm. You'll beat yourself up afterward. You'll feel like you're back where you started.

But you're not. Because the difference now is that you *know* what's happening, you *see* the pattern. You *understand* the reaction. And that alone creates space for something new.

You don't erase years of conditioning in a single week. But now and then, you say, no matter how shaky, you plant a seed. Every breath you take is tainted by guilt, which rewires your inner world. Every time you hold a boundary without self-abandoning, you reclaim a piece of yourself that once felt lost.

In the next segment, we'll reframe the idea of "no" as an act of love, not just for yourself, but for others. Because when your "no" is grounded, honest, and kind, it doesn't burn bridges; it builds truth.

Saying No as a Loving Act

Most people associate saying no with rejection. That's why it feels so hard. In the back of your mind, or maybe right at the front, there's a whisper that says: *If I say no, I'm pushing them away. If I say no, I'm not being loving. If I say no, I'm closing the door.*

But that's not what's happening.

When you say no from alignment, from presence, from honesty, from your center, you're not rejecting anyone. You're refusing to lie. And refusing to lie is one of the most loving things you can do.

Because love without truth is not sustainable.

We've been trained to believe that love requires sacrifice. And to a degree, it does; no relationship exists without some measure of compromise, of give and take. But there's a difference between conscious sacrifice and unconscious self-abandonment. There's a difference between choosing to show up for someone out of desire and feeling unable to say no out of guilt.

In the first case, love thrives. In the second, it slowly erodes.

Saying yes when you mean no may keep someone else comfortable in the short term, but it makes you disappear in the process. Over time, that disappearance turns into resentment. And resentment is far more corrosive than any honest no.

When you say no with love, what you're doing is saying yes to truth, to mutual respect, to your wellbeing. You're inviting the other person to meet you in reality, not in projection or obligation. You're saying: *I care enough about this connection not to contaminate it with my silent resentment.*

That's not cruelty. That's maturity.

Still, there's often fear that your no will hurt someone. And sometimes it will. Sometimes people will be disappointed. But here's the thing about disappointment: it's not fatal. It's survivable. And it's *not the same* as harm.

This distinction is essential.

Many of us collapse the two. We think: *If I disappoint them, I'm causing harm.* But disappointment is a natural and necessary part of adult relationships. You cannot live honestly without sometimes letting people down. And when you avoid disappointment at all costs, you don't build trust; you make a persona.

Your job is not to prevent disappointment. Your job is to communicate with care and to stand in your truth with as much compassion as you can.

That's the sweet spot.

A kind of. A grounded number. A no that doesn't flinch, doesn't punish, doesn't over justify. Just clear. Respectful. Firm.

This kind of no becomes a gift. Not always in the moment, it might sting at first, but in the long run, it creates something far more meaningful than perpetual agreement: it creates *clarity*. And clarity, unlike comfort, is what lets a relationship breathe.

It lets people trust your yes. It allows them to relax around you because they know where you stand. They don't have to guess. They don't have to manage your emotions. They don't have to wonder whether you want to be there.

You're not teaching people how to genuinely love you, not just how to use your availability.

And it teaches *you* how to love others without losing yourself.

It's important to say here that not every no is kind, just like not every yes is. Delivery matters. Timing matters. Your tone, your presence, and your posture all speak just as loudly as your words. A defensive no comes from fear. A sharp no comes from unhealed resentment. A vague no comes from confusion. But a loving, no, firm, clear, calm, comes from knowing yourself.

That's the muscle we're building: the ability to stay in your truth without closing your heart.

You might not get it right every time. That's okay. Sometimes you'll overcorrect. Sometimes you'll set a boundary too late and explode instead of speaking calmly. Sometimes you'll backtrack because the guilt is too intense. These moments are not failures.

Their feedback. They're proof that you're learning, recalibrating, growing into your full shape.

With practice, you'll begin to notice the moments when your no *is* love.

When you say no to a commitment, it gives someone else a chance to step up. Saying no to an unhealthy pattern makes space for healing, and saying no to a draining dynamic preserves a relationship that otherwise would've broken under pressure. Saying no to what you're not available for allows you to fully say yes to what you are.

And that's the point.

Saying no isn't about being rigid or aloof or unavailable. It's about being *honest*. It's about being trustworthy, not because you always agree, but because you show up with integrity.

In the next segment, we'll begin translating this internal clarity into external practice. You'll work with journal prompts that help you map your emotional patterns, identify your most persistent guilt triggers, and prepare to rewrite them with intention.

Because the more you see what's running your no, the more power you have to choose something different.

Seeing Your Emotional Patterns Clearly

Most people don't realize they're living according to emotional scripts until the script fails them. They overlook the reflexive guilt until they say no and spend the next three hours replaying it in their mind. They don't question the fear until they realize their friendships are built more on obligation than joy.

They don't recognize their avoidance of boundaries until they burn out or blow up, too late to choose differently.

But all of this can change. And it starts by seeing clearly.

Noticing is the first disruption. Naming is the second. Once you name a pattern, you gain power over it. It becomes something you can respond to rather than react to. That's what this part of the work is about: slowing down the automatic reflex of guilt and replacing it with reflection, agency, and choice.

You don't need to be a seasoned journaler or a highly self-aware person to begin this. All you need is honesty and a willingness to listen to yourself without judgment. The stories you've internalized didn't start with you, but they can end with you.

Start with a simple question: When do I feel guilty saying no?

Notice the specifics. Is it when you say no to your parents? To your manager? To your partner? Does guilt show up when you decline a social event? When you refuse a favor? What happens when you don't return a message right away?

Look for patterns. You might realize that your guilt isn't about the action itself, but about who's involved. Perhaps you were taught that family always comes first, so saying no to a sibling feels like betrayal. Or maybe you were praised for being helpful at work, so not volunteering for extra tasks feels like a moral failure.

Each instance of guilt carries a message. Write them out:

> ➤ What did I say no to?
> ➤ Who was involved?
> ➤ What did I feel in my body afterward?
> ➤ What thoughts followed that feeling?

> ➤ What was I afraid would happen because of my no?

This exercise can be confronting. You might uncover stories you didn't know were running your decisions. You might feel anger at yourself, at others, at the years you've spent saying yes when you didn't mean it. That's okay. Let it surface. Let the truth land without rushing to make it prettier than it is.

Then, gently ask: What is the story I'm telling myself about why I can't say no?

Here are some common ones:

> ➤ If I say no, I'm a bad friend.
> ➤ If I say no, I'll lose the opportunity.
> ➤ If I say no, they'll think I don't care.
> ➤ If I say no, I'm selfish.
> ➤ If I say no, I'll be alone.

Each of these beliefs carries emotional weight, but that doesn't mean they're true. Many of them were inherited or imprinted early. You were taught to believe these things by experience, not evidence. Beliefs formed in survival are not always helpful in thriving.

Now, rewrite the story.

This doesn't mean creating a fantasy. It means constructing a new script based on your current values and truth.

Here's how that looks:

> ➤ Old belief: If I say no, I'm rejecting them.
> ➤ New truth: If I say no with care, I'm honoring both of us.
> ➤ Old belief: Saying no makes me selfish.
> ➤ New truth: Saying no makes me honest, which is the foundation of genuine generosity.

➢ Old belief: If I set a boundary, they'll leave.

➢ New truth: If someone leaves because I set a boundary, the relationship was conditional, and I deserve better.

This rewriting is not just semantic. It's reprogramming. It's your brain, heart, and body learning to relate to truth in a new way. And the more you practice it, the more automatic it becomes.

As you do this work, notice how your body reacts. Where do you feel tension when you write your old story? Where do you think the release is when you speak the new one?

You may discover that your guilt isn't a stop sign; it's just a familiar ghost. Something that shows up when you're stretching into new territory. Not to punish you, but to remind you that you're no longer living in the old contract.

And remember, guilt doesn't always need to be erased. Sometimes, it just needs to be held and acknowledged and witnessed without giving it the power to steer.

Because guilt only has power when it's unexamined.

When it's illuminated, on the page, in your voice, through reflection, it becomes something you can walk beside. Something you can breathe through. Something that no longer stops you.

In the next and final segment of this chapter, we'll create a blueprint for how to move forward, how to carry your no with confidence, use it as a tool for care, and trust yourself even when old fears arise. You'll come away with a felt sense that guilt is not your enemy, and that your boundaries, no matter how new, are building something beautiful.

Carrying Your No with Confidence

If you've come this far, you already know something profound and essential: saying no isn't the end of connection, it's the beginning of truth. But knowing it in your mind and living it in your body are different things. The work now is to move from awareness to embodiment, to carry your no into the world not as a weapon, not as a shield, but as a practice of self-respect.

No, when spoken with love, is a gift. It may not feel like one in the moment. It may still be wrapped in fear, guilt, or vulnerability. But it is still a gift, both to you and to the person you say it to. Because it brings clarity. And clarity, over time, creates safety.

Still, it helps to be prepared for the fire.

The fire is the flash of anxiety that comes after you decline. The discomfort of watching someone react. The temptation to backtrack. The reflex to soften, explain, or overcompensate. It's normal. It's predictable. It's just part of the change process. Don't be afraid of it. Please don't take it as a sign that something's gone wrong. It's simply the nervous system catching up to the new script.

When the fire comes, your job is not to avoid it, but to stay present with it. Ground yourself. Breathe low. Reaffirm the truth: *This is unfamiliar, not unsafe. This is uncomfortable, not unkind.* You are not doing something wrong. You are doing something *new*.

The people around you may need time, too. If they are used to your automatic yes, your boundaries may feel like distance, even rejection. That doesn't mean you should adjust your boundary; it means you communicate it with care.

You can say:

> ➤ "I know I used to always say yes to this, and I care about you. But I've realized I need to make a change."
> ➤ "This isn't about pulling away. It's about staying in integrity."
> ➤ "It matters to me that we stay connected, and I also need to take care of myself differently now."

You don't owe anyone a long explanation, but sometimes, a little context can build a bridge. It can soften the edges. It can remind the person on the other end that your no is not about punishment. It's about truth.

And truth, ultimately, is what deepens relationships, not ruins them.

It's worth saying here: some relationships won't survive your no. Some people will not adapt. They'll withdraw, guilt you, or even lash out. This is painful. And yet, these moments are clarifying. They reveal the unspoken contracts you've been keeping, contracts that only held as long as you kept abandoning yourself.

But a relationship that can't hold your truth is not a relationship. It's a performance.

You're not burning bridges. It's revealing which bridges were real, and which were built on your silence.

There will also be people who surprise you. People who thank you for your honesty. People who adjust. People who may not get it right away, but who come back around, ready to meet the new version of you. These are your people. Keep them close. Not because they always agree, but because they're willing to grow with you.

Over time, your no becomes less dramatic. Less charged. It becomes something steady and straightforward. A regular part of your vocabulary. A boundary drawn not in defensiveness, but in clarity.

You'll notice it in how you respond to requests. In how you move through your calendar. In how you speak in meetings, to your partner, or to your family. You'll feel it in the space between impulse and action. In the pause. The breath. The moment when you check in with yourself before answering.

That pause is power. That breath is freedom.

Because you are no longer reacting from guilt. You are responding to the truth.

Your nervous system will begin to adjust. Your inner child will feel safer. Your adult self will stand taller. Your life will start to feel like it belongs to you again, not just in theory, but in practice.

And that's the point of this chapter, not to eliminate guilt or make fear vanish completely. But to help you build the strength to carry on anyway. To stay connected to your values, even when your body protests. To walk through the fire, not because you enjoy it, but because you're no longer willing to burn *yourself* to keep everyone else warm.

The guilt may still come. But now you know what to do with it.

Breathe. Soften. Remind yourself: This is new. This is necessary. This is love.

Now that we've addressed the emotional blocks that hold many of us back, it's time to equip you with the words, tone, and confidence to say no clearly and kindly.

With emotional blocks beginning to loosen, it's time to put theory into practice. How do you say no clearly and kindly without falling into passivity or aggression? Chapter 6 offers the language, tone, and techniques to communicate your boundaries with confidence and grace.

In the next chapter, we'll shift into language. You'll learn how to speak your no out loud, not just internally. You'll be given tools, tone work, and real-world scripts to say no clearly, kindly, and without the weight of over-explaining. Because boundaries begin inside you, but they live in your voice.

Chapter 6: Reclaiming Your Voice

You've done the inner work. You've dismantled the guilt. You've rewritten the old stories. You've even begun feeling where your boundaries live inside your body. But now comes the real-world test: using your voice.

Because a boundary is only as strong as your willingness to express it, you can have the clearest internal compass, the most profound conviction, but until your "no" leaves your mouth, it lives in theory, not reality.

This is where many people get stuck.

They know they need to say no, but they freeze. They avoid. They wait. They try to hint, suggest, or disappear, hoping the issue will resolve itself. And when it doesn't, they either over-explain or explode. They swing between silence and defensiveness, trying to walk a tightrope between being clear and being liked.

But here's the truth: saying no doesn't require perfection. It requires practice.

And that practice begins with understanding the kind of communicator you've been trained to be.

Most people operate from one of three dominant styles: passive, aggressive, or assertive.

Passive communicators avoid conflict at all costs. They say yes when they mean no. They soften their language, defer their needs, and often apologize for simply having an opinion. They hope that if they're nice enough, they won't be pushed or abandoned. But passivity usually leads to precisely what it's trying to avoid: disconnection. Because unspoken needs don't go away, they turn into resentment.

Aggressive communicators swing to the opposite end. Their tone is clear, but sharp. They often speak from defensiveness before fully thinking. They believe boundaries require confrontation, and so their energy carries tension even when their words are accurate. This style can protect them, but it often damages relationships, creating fear rather than respect.

Then there's assertiveness. This is the gold standard, but not because it's louder or more convincing. Assertive communication is calm, direct, and emotionally grounded. It comes from a place of clarity, not control. An assertive "no" doesn't attack or collapse. It simply stands.

For those who were raised without models of assertive communication, this can feel like a foreign language. But it's a language that can be learned. The first step is to understand what makes an assertive no different.

It's not about volume. It's not about dominating a conversation or always getting your way. It's about ownership. Assertive people speak from their experience. They don't over-explain or accuse. They don't try to convince others of their worth. They share what is true for them, without apology.

This is not always easy. Assertiveness requires you to tolerate the discomfort of someone else not liking your answer. It requires you to hold your center even when someone pushes back. It requires the maturity to say, "I understand that you're disappointed. And my answer is still no."

This level of confidence doesn't happen overnight. It's built through repetition, through hundreds of small choices to speak with more honesty, more clarity, and less self-editing.

And it starts in low-stakes moments.

When a coworker asks, "Do you have a minute?" you pause, check in with yourself, and say, "I can't talk right now, can we check in after lunch?"

When a friend asks, "Are you free this weekend?" you take a breath and say, "I'm keeping my weekend open for rest, but I'd love to find another time soon."

When someone pushes, "Come on, it's not a big deal," you respond with, "It might not feel like a big deal to you, but it is to me, and I'm standing by my decision."

These small conversations build your muscle. They show your nervous system that saying no doesn't end in exile. They rewire your body to understand that discomfort isn't danger. And they begin to teach the people around you how to relate to the *real* you, not just the agreeable version they've gotten used to.

It's crucial here to acknowledge that not every no will be received with grace. Some people will challenge you. Some will question your motives. Some will try to guilt, pressure, or test you. That's not a failure. That's just what happens when you stop playing a role.

Your job isn't to control their reaction. Your job is to stay rooted in your intention.

That's why tone matters so much. Not just what you say, but how you say it. Assertiveness lives in the middle ground. You're not backing down, but you're not escalating either. You're clear, calm, and anchored. You're not defending your no, you're simply delivering it.

This energy, what some call "neutral firmness", is what gives your words weight without making them heavy. You're not trying to be liked. You're trying to be clear. And over time, people begin to trust that energy. Even if they don't always agree with you, they know what to expect; they know you won't be swayed by pressure, nor will you retaliate with drama.

You become steady. Predictable in the best way. Boundaried and still kind.

In the next segment, we'll dive into the mechanics of how to say no, what to say, how to say it, and how to read the moment so that your delivery fits the dynamic. Because as much as boundary-setting is an inner decision, it's also an outer skill. And like any skill, it gets better with use.

Finding the Words, Saying No in Real Time

Knowing you need to say no is one thing. Saying it, out loud, in the moment, with a steady voice, is another. This is where many people hesitate, not because they don't understand the value of a boundary, but because they're unsure how to communicate it without sounding defensive, cold, or rude.

The fear often isn't about saying no. It's about what will happen *after* you say it.

Will the person be hurt? Will they push back? Will they think you're selfish? Will you suddenly forget how to stand your ground?

This is why preparation matters. Not just emotional readiness, but actual language. Words you can use. Sentences you can practice. Structures that help you speak clearly when the moment comes.

And let's be clear: the moment *will* come.

Someone will ask for your time. Your energy. Your availability. And in that instant, your brain will want to revert to the familiar, to please, to agree, to smooth things over. But if you've already rehearsed how to say no, if you've already worked the muscle, the boundary doesn't have to be improvised. It becomes accessible. You can reach for the script, deliver it with care, and move on without collapsing into guilt.

Start with this idea: a clear no does not require an elaborate justification.

You might think, *I have to explain why I can't do it. I need to make sure they understand.* But often, the longer you explain, the more it sounds like you're asking permission, or worse, like your no is negotiable.

You don't owe anyone your whole calendar. You don't have to defend your bandwidth. You only need to state the truth with clarity and kindness.

A simple, direct no might sound like:
- "Thanks for thinking of me, but I'm not available for that."
- "I can't commit to that right now."
- "That's not something I can say yes to, but I hope it goes well."

If this feels too abrupt, you can soften the delivery without compromising the message:

> ➤ "I appreciate the invite. I need to pass this time, but thank you for including me."
> ➤ "That sounds like a great cause, but I'm not taking on anything new at the moment."
> ➤ "I know this matters to you, and I want to be honest, I can't take this on right now."

The key is to anchor the "no" early in the sentence. Many people bury their refusal under layers of apology or delay. They say, "Well, I'd love to, but I'm kind of swamped…" or "Maybe next time," or "Let me get back to you", when they already know the answer is no.

This kind of ambiguity breeds confusion. It signals that your no is fragile, that with enough pressure, it might become a yes. And for people who are used to you always saying yes, that ambiguity is an invitation to push.

Clarity is kinder than ambiguity.

When you speak clearly, you set the expectation. You stop the back-and-forth before it begins. And even if the person is disappointed, they'll usually respect the boundary if the delivery is respectful and confident.

That's where tone becomes your ally.

A boundary delivered with anxiety invites negotiation. A boundary delivered with resentment triggers defensiveness. But a boundary delivered with calm presence? That lands. Even if someone doesn't like what they hear, they'll feel the difference between rejection and respect.

If you struggle to find your assertive tone, try practicing with your breath. A low, grounded breath naturally supports a more relaxed voice. Stand tall, plant your feet, and rehearse your phrases aloud, not just once, but repeatedly. Build the muscle memory. So, when the real moment comes, your voice doesn't betray you. It backs you up.

You can also prepare for different types of nos. There's the gentle decline, the firm refusal, the redirect, and the boundary around repeated behavior.

A gentle decline might sound like: "I appreciate the offer, but I'm not available."

A firm refusal might sound like: "That doesn't work for me."

A redirect could be: "I can't help with that, but I'd be happy to point you to someone else."

And a behavioral boundary, when someone continues to overstep, might sound like: "We've had this conversation before, and I want to be clear: I'm not available for that, and I need you to respect that going forward."

All of these are valid. You don't need to pick just one tone for life. The best communicators are flexible; they adjust their language and delivery based on the context, without abandoning their truth.

Some conversations will require you to be gentle. Others will need more edge. Some will be casual and easy. Others will test everything you've practiced.

But the more you say no, the less intense it becomes. Not because the world changes, but because *you* do. You stop fearing the discomfort. You stop over-correcting for the other person's emotions. You realize that your job isn't to control their reaction, it's to communicate your truth.

In the next segment, we'll explore how to read social dynamics, how to know when to soften your tone, when to stand firm, and how to navigate nuance without falling back into over-accommodation. Because saying no well isn't just about the words. It's about the moment, the energy, the intention.

Knowing When to Soften or Stand Firm

There's no single "right way" to say no. Boundaries are not one-size-fits-all. The way you communicate them will, and should, shift depending on who you're talking to, what's at stake, and the emotional tone of the moment. This isn't about being inconsistent. It's about being emotionally intelligent.

Some no's require softness. Some require steel. And the skill you're building isn't just the ability to *say* no, it's the ability to *read* the moment and choose the most effective way to deliver it.

Emotional intelligence doesn't mean you mold yourself to meet everyone's expectations. It means you're attuned enough to others and yourself to understand when flexibility in tone supports the outcome and when firmness is necessary to avoid confusion or enable clarity.

Let's start with the moments that benefit from a softer delivery.

Imagine a friend asks for a favor, something you would've said yes to in the past, but no longer have the capacity for. They're not demanding. They're not pressuring. They ask, expecting your usual yes. This is a moment for warmth, not edge. You might say, "I'd love to help, and I want to be honest, I've got too much on my plate right now. I care about you, and I don't want to take this on and drop the ball."

You're not apologizing for the no. You're simply wrapping it in care.

Now, contrast that with a situation where someone is overstepping. Maybe a colleague keeps assigning tasks that aren't yours. Or a relative is pushing you to attend an event you've already declined. This is where clarity must take priority over comfort. The person has already shown they may not take a hint. In this case, your tone might shift to something firmer: "I've said no, and I need you to respect that decision." Not cruel. Not confrontational. Just anchored.

Tone is your tool, not your enemy. And you don't need to perform to use it.

Many people who struggle with boundaries fear firmness because they associate it with aggression. They worry they'll be seen as rude, mean, or cold. But firmness, when delivered from a grounded place, doesn't mean it's clean. It removes ambiguity. It reduces resentment. It teaches people how to treat you in the future.

What's often misunderstood is that being "too nice" in your delivery can create more discomfort, not less. A sugar-coated no can confuse people. They hear all the sweetness and think, *Maybe she'll change her mind.* Or *maybe I need to ask again later.* They don't realize they've just heard a boundary, because the language was too vague or tentative.

That's not clarity. That's avoidance.

Clarity isn't unkind. It's a relief. Even when people don't like your answer, they usually appreciate your directness, especially if you deliver it without defensiveness or apology.

It's also important to recognize when your tone is being influenced by fear.

Fear shows up in your voice when you doubt your right to say no. It creeps into your language as hesitation: "I'm sorry, but I don't think I can…" or "I mean, if that's okay…" or "I feel bad, but I just don't want to be a burden…"

This kind of delivery trains people to assume your boundaries are flexible. And worse, it reinforces the belief in *you* that you don't need permission to be valid.

You don't need to apologize for your needs.

You don't need to phrase every no as if it's a personal failure.

You don't need to shrink when you speak your truth.

If you're unsure how your tone is landing, try practicing aloud. Record yourself. Say your boundary three different ways — soft, neutral, and firm — and listen back. Which version sounds the most like your authentic voice? Which one makes you feel steady, not small?

The goal isn't to sound like someone else. It's to find *your* clear voice, the one that holds your boundaries with integrity, without leaning too far toward harshness or hiding.

There's also the social context to consider.

Is this a workplace situation with a power dynamic? Is this a family setting where roles are deeply entrenched? Is this a friendship where patterns have formed over the years?

In professional settings, clarity matters more than emotion. You can be friendly, but your primary job is to be direct and reliable. "I can't take that on right now. Let's talk about a reasonable timeline," is more effective than, "I'm feeling overwhelmed, and I just don't know if I can do this."

In personal relationships, tone and language often matter more than speed. You may need to slow down, make space for emotion, and reinforce the relationship as you set the boundary: "I care about you so much, and I want to be honest because I value our connection. I don't have the capacity for that right now."

It's not manipulation, it's relational fluency.

It's knowing your audience, not to people-please, but to create the best chance of your boundary being received without unnecessary rupture.

And even then, some people won't respond well. No amount of careful tone or thoughtful phrasing will make sure people respect your boundary. And when that happens, it's not a failure in delivery. It's a signal about the relationship.

Boundaries are a filter. Not everyone makes it through. That's not cruelty. That's clarity doing its job.

In the next segment, we'll focus on building muscle through repetition. You'll get practical exercises and scenarios to rehearse your no, refine your tone, and prepare yourself for those "in the moment" tests that often catch people off guard. Because confidence isn't something you summon, it's something you build, one boundary at a time.

Repetition Builds Confidence, Practicing Your No

Clarity isn't a personality trait; it's a practice. And like any practice, it improves with repetition. You don't learn how to say no by thinking about it. You learn by *doing* it. Again, and again.

In small moments, awkward conversations, quick declines, and firm refusals that begin to teach your nervous system: *This is safe. This is allowed. This is who I am now.*

This segment is about helping you build that muscle.

You don't need to wait for a high-stakes boundary situation to start practicing. Those are the hardest places to begin. Start where the pressure is lower, where saying no won't unravel a relationship, disappoint a parent, or challenge a decades-old pattern. Start small and start now.

Begin by choosing five real-life scenarios you face regularly. Things like:

➢ Being asked to stay late at work.
➢ Getting invited to a social gathering you don't want to attend.
➢ Being asked for a favor that would stretch your time or energy.
➢ Receiving a last-minute call or text, expecting immediate engagement.
➢ Being pulled into a conversation or conflict you didn't initiate.

For each one, write out how you usually respond. Be honest. Do you say yes and resent it later? Do you hesitate, but give in? Do you ghost the situation entirely, hoping it will resolve itself?

Now rewrite your response. Not as the person you've been, but as the version of you that honors boundaries. Use assertive, respectful, clear language. Aim for brevity and strength. Something like:

➢ "I won't be able to stay late today; I have a hard stop at five."

> ➤ "Thanks for the invite, but I'm planning on staying in this weekend."
> ➤ "I wish I could help, but I'm at capacity right now."
> ➤ "I can't respond immediately, but I'll check in later when I have space."
> ➤ "I'm not available to talk about that right now."

Now practice saying these phrases out loud. Yes, out loud. You can't skip the vocal step. The voice carries not just words, but energy. The way your boundary sounds *to you* matters. It needs to feel like something your body can support, not just something your brain approves of.

If you stumble or feel awkward at first, that's normal. Your vocal cords are used for softer, more compliant language. They've been trained to phrase requests as apologies. That will shift, through repetition.

Try saying each boundary five times in a row. Notice how your tone evolves. Notice what happens in your posture. Your breath. Your body.

Are you rushing through the sentence? Are you pitching your voice upward, turning a statement into a question? Are you trailing off, shrinking at the end? If so, slow down. Speak from your chest, not your throat. Imagine your words landing clearly on the other person's side of the conversation, not ricocheting off guilt or fear.

This kind of rehearsal is not about memorizing scripts. It's about teaching your nervous system that your no is safe to express. And the more you practice it in neutral or safe environments, the easier it becomes to access in higher-pressure moments.

Next, take it one step further: ask a trusted friend to role-play with you. Choose a few boundary scenarios and take turns acting them out. Practice delivering your no with presence while your friend offers different responses, acceptance, disappointment, and even subtle pushback. Then switch roles.

Notice how much easier it becomes to hold your ground when you've already felt the fear in a low-stakes setting. Role-playing like this is not childish; it's rehearsal for adulthood done right.

The more you practice your "no," the more naturally it will surface when you need it.

What once felt like a confrontation becomes a simple conversation. What once felt like a risk becomes routine. You'll begin to notice the space between stimulus and response, those few precious seconds where you get to decide who you are and how you want to show up.

That space is everything.

In the past, you may have filled that space with fear, overthinking, or compliance. But now, you fill it with pause. With breath. With intention. You let your no come from a centered place, not a reactive one. And that kind of no is powerful. Not because it's loud, but because it's honest.

It doesn't need to convince. It doesn't need to justify. It doesn't need to perform.

It simply stands.

This is what repetition gives you, not just skill, but self-trust. You begin to believe your no isn't something you have to *earn* the right to say. It's simply a part of your vocabulary. A tool for truth. A marker of maturity.

In the next segment, we'll help you personalize these skills even further. You'll be invited to write your scripts for five real-life situations, ones you've struggled with or anticipate facing, because it's not enough to prepare for the *general* challenge of saying no. You need language tailored to *your* life, your voice, and your values.

Crafting Personal Scripts for Real Life

Repetition builds fluency. But *relevance* builds confidence. It's not enough to practice generic no's in a vacuum; you have to speak into the actual moments that challenge you. The texts you avoid. The invitations you feel too guilty to decline. The coworker who asks for "just one more thing." The family member who assumes you'll always say yes.

This is the part of the work where we get personal.

You're going to write your scripts, not to memorize, not to recite like a robot, but to ground yourself. When you've already written it once, saying it out loud later becomes less terrifying. You're not searching for the words while your anxiety rises. You've got a foundation to stand on.

Choose five real situations from your life. If you're not sure where to start, scan your calendar, your inbox, and your text threads. Find the moments where you said yes and then regretted it, or where you said nothing and carried the weight anyway.

For each, you'll answer three questions:

1. Be specific. "A friend always calls late at night expecting me to talk," or "My boss adds tasks at the

last minute on Fridays," or "I get invited to every extended family function and feel bad skipping."

2. Not what you think you

3. Be able to tolerate, but what you need. "I don't want to talk on the phone after 9 PM." "I want at least 48 hours' notice for new assignments." "I want to say yes to family events selectively, not automatically."

4. This is your script. Think of the actual words you'd use, not lofty affirmations, but practical sentences that feel like your voice. Direct but not harsh. Clear but not cold.

Here's what it looks like in practice:

Scenario 1: Your friend keeps inviting you to spontaneous plans, expecting an instant yes.

Boundary: I want to stop saying yes out of pressure and have the freedom to decline without guilt.

Script: "I appreciate the invite, but I've learned I do better with a little notice. I won't be joining this time, but let's find a day that works ahead of time."

Scenario 2: Your boss frequently asks you to "just take a quick look" at things on your day off.

Boundary: I want my time off to be protected without having to explain myself each time.

Script: "I'm offline today and can't review this right now. Let's connect when I'm back in."

Scenario 3: A family member keeps asking you to help with errands or childcare without checking your schedule.

Boundary: I need to stop rearranging my life at the last minute to accommodate their needs.

Script: "I'm not available that day, and I need more notice for these kinds of requests. I hope you're able to find another option."

Scenario 4: A friend sends emotional venting texts at all hours and expects an immediate response.

Boundary: I want to be a supportive friend without being emotionally available 24/7.

Script: "I care about you, and I also need to protect my capacity. I'll read your message when I have space, but I can't always respond right away."

Scenario 5: A client keeps calling after hours and bypassing email boundaries.

Boundary: I want to set clear work-life boundaries and not be reactive to every ping.

Script: "For future communication, please send requests via email during business hours. I check messages during that time and will get back to you as soon as I'm available."

Once you've created your own five, speak to them aloud. Practice with a neutral face and tone. Then tell them as if you're talking to the actual person. You might feel tension or nerves rise, especially if these relationships are emotionally charged. Let that happen. Don't avoid it. It's part of the recalibration process.

The goal here is not perfection. It's preparedness. When you've written these scripts and rehearsed them, your mind is less likely to go blank when you're in a real conversation. You've already paved a mental path. You've already made space in your nervous system for clarity.

What if you try a script and it doesn't land well? What if you say it and the person pushes back?

Then you stand by it.

You don't need to escalate. You don't need to argue. You repeat the boundary calmly. If they say, "I just don't understand why you can't," you can respond, "I hear that this is disappointing, and I've made my decision." Let that be enough.

This is where your power grows, not from volume, but from steadiness.

Remember, you are not trying to convince. You're not trying to be bulletproof. You're trying to be honest.

And the most honest thing you can say sometimes is, "I can't do that." Not because you don't care. But because you've stopped abandoning yourself to meet everyone else's comfort.

In the next and final segment of this chapter, we'll bring all of this together. You'll reflect on what you've practiced and prepare yourself for the inevitable reality: some boundaries will be tested. We'll walk through how to respond when someone pushes back, so your "no" stays grounded, even when challenged.

When No Meets Resistance

Saying no is a profound act of self-respect, but it often invites resistance. People accustomed to your yes might be surprised, hurt, or even angry when you shift your pattern. The moment your no is met with pushback can feel like a test, a challenge, or a threat to connection.

This is where many boundaries falter, not because the boundary itself is wrong, but because the person setting it doesn't know how to hold firm in the face of discomfort.

First, it helps to remember that resistance is a natural reaction. It's human to want what you want. It's human to feel disappointed when you don't get it. And sometimes, people push back, not out of malice, but out of habit, fear, or unmet needs of their own.

Your job isn't to make their discomfort disappear. Your job is to stay steady.

Here's a simple framework for holding your ground with care:

1. You can say, "I hear that this is frustrating for you," or "I understand this isn't what you hoped for." This shows empathy and keeps the connection open.

2. Follow your acknowledgment with, "But my answer remains the same," or "And I need to stick with my decision."

3. Resist the urge to give a long list of reasons. The more you explain, the more your boundary sounds negotiable.

4. For example, "I need to protect my time right now," or "I'm not able to take that on." This keeps the

conversation about your limits rather than their demands.

5. You might say, "I want to continue this conversation when we can both be calm," or "I'm going to step away now, and we can talk later if needed."

By practicing these steps, you transform pushback from a battleground into a conversation about respect. You model how to hold a boundary without hostility, and collapse.

It's also important to accept that some resistance won't soften. Some people will try to guilt you, pressure you, or dismiss your boundary. When that happens, remind yourself that your boundary is a gift to yourself, not a weapon against them.

If the relationship can't hold you without disrespect, that's a red flag. Boundaries reveal true colors. And protecting your peace means sometimes letting go of those who can't meet you with respect.

Holding firm also means practicing self-compassion. It's normal to feel guilty or anxious when someone pushes back. You might second-guess yourself or worry about damaging the relationship. When that happens, return to your core truths:

➢ Saying no is my right.
➢ My needs are valid.
➢ I can care about others without sacrificing myself.
➢ Discomfort is temporary; self-respect is lasting.

Over time, these affirmations become easier to embody. Your no becomes your boundary's strongest armor, not because it's loud, but because it's steady.

And this steadiness is the foundation of healthy, honest relationships. Relationships that don't ask you to disappear but invite you to show up fully. Relationships where no means no and yes means yes.

Remember: saying no is not about burning bridges. It's about building them from a place of truth. When you say no clearly and kindly, you create space for genuine connection, a connection that doesn't require sacrifice but thrives on integrity.

In the chapters ahead, we'll explore how to take these skills into specific areas of your life, work, family, friendships, and even your relationship with yourself. Each context has its nuances, but the core remains the same: your voice matters, your boundaries matter, and your no is sacred.

Chapter 7: The Unspoken Work Contract

Why Boundaries at Work Matter

Walking into a workplace, whether an office buzzing with collaboration, a quiet remote setup, or the unpredictable world of client-facing roles, you quickly discover an unspoken contract governing your time, energy, and availability. This contract, rarely written down but deeply felt, shapes not only how you perform but also how you are perceived, valued, and ultimately, sustained.

Most people start their careers eager to prove their worth. They readily agree, stretch themselves thin, and believe that showing commitment means accepting every task. Early enthusiasm can be mistaken for unlimited availability, and with time, that assumption becomes a hard expectation others lean on. Overcommitment creeps in slowly, like water through cracks in a foundation, until fatigue sets in and the cracks widen.

At work, boundaries are both more necessary and more challenging than in other spheres. Why? Because professional relationships often come wrapped in layers of hierarchy, mixed motives, and power dynamics that can confuse and complicate the act of saying no. Saying no to a colleague might feel risky, but saying no to a boss, a client, or a company culture that prizes "always on" dedication can feel nearly impossible.

This chapter peels back the layers of those unspoken expectations. It explores why drawing lines at work is critical, not just for your mental health, but for your professional reputation and long-term success.

When boundaries are unclear or absent, work hours bleed into personal time, projects multiply without clear limits, and small "quick favors" turn into massive undertakings without recognition or compensation. Burnout becomes an ever-present shadow, creativity stagnates, and what began as enthusiasm morphs into resentment. People start to dread mornings, their workspaces, and even their careers.

The pressure to be constantly available is heightened in the era of remote work and digital connectivity. The ping of an email or message after hours is no longer an exception but an expectation. Clients ask for "just one more thing" with a casualness that masks the real cost. Managers push deadlines tighter without checking in on bandwidth. Teammates lean heavily on those known for saying yes, creating an invisible labor imbalance.

These dynamics breed a silent epidemic of exhaustion. The workday never truly ends, and neither does the feeling that you should be doing more. But the truth is, without boundaries, your professional life will not be sustainable. You may get by in the short term, but eventually, something gives: your health, your relationships, your sense of purpose.

Setting boundaries at work isn't just about saying no. It's about protecting the quality and integrity of your contributions. It's about saying yes to what aligns with your goals and values, and no to what detracts from them. It's about reclaiming your time and energy so you can bring your best self to your work and the people you serve.

However, this is easier said than done. Workplaces often reward overextension, sometimes even confuse busyness with productivity. It takes courage and strategy to push back without jeopardizing your standing. It requires you to understand the nuances of professional communication, to anticipate resistance, and to craft your boundaries in ways that command respect rather than invite backlash.

In this chapter, we'll walk through the complexities of workplace boundaries. You'll hear stories of people who learned the hard way and how they found balance. You'll gain tools for identifying scope creep, negotiating limits, and managing expectations with managers, clients, and colleagues. You'll learn scripts and techniques for saying no with grace and firmness, and how to maintain your boundaries even when the culture around you pushes against them.

Most importantly, you'll discover that holding boundaries at work is not a rejection of professionalism or commitment. It's the foundation of both. When you create space for yourself, you make space for excellence. When you protect your time, you protect your reputation. When you say no thoughtfully, you say yes to your career's longevity and your well-being.

The work world may expect you to be endlessly available, but you don't have to accept that. Your career can thrive, your relationships at work can deepen, and your creative fire can burn bright, all because you choose to draw the lines that honor your humanity.

In the next segment, we'll explore practical strategies to recognize and prevent scope creep, the subtle and sometimes blatant expansion of your workload beyond your original role. Understanding this phenomenon is key to setting the boundaries that keep your professional life manageable and meaningful.

Recognizing and Preventing Scope Creep

Scope creep often begins as a subtle shift, almost imperceptible at first. You might find yourself agreeing to a small additional task here or an extra favor there, each seemingly insignificant on its own. But over weeks or months, these small asks accumulate, expanding your workload beyond what was initially intended or agreed upon. The problem with scope creep isn't just the added volume of work; it's the way it chips away at your clarity and control, gradually pulling you away from your core responsibilities and leaving you feeling overwhelmed, undervalued, and exhausted.

Imagine a project that initially sparked your enthusiasm, one where your role was well-defined and your deadlines reasonable. Then, almost without warning, a new request arrives, a tweak here, a last-minute addition there, presented as a minor favor or a quick fix. Wanting to be helpful or to avoid conflict, you accept. But these seemingly small shifts keep coming, each one quietly expanding your obligations while the expectations around compensation, time, or resources remain unchanged.

This is the silent erosion of boundaries. It's a familiar scenario for many who strive to prove their dedication or who hesitate to refuse for fear of disappointing others. Scope creep does more than overburden your schedule; it blurs the lines between your responsibilities and those of others, transforming you into a catch-all for tasks beyond your original remit. Your days fill with reactive work, diminishing the time and mental space available for creative, strategic efforts or even rest.

Recognizing scope creep before it overwhelms you requires attentive awareness. Often, it reveals itself in the language used around you: phrases like "Could you just...," "This will only take a minute," or "I know this isn't in your role, but..." These subtle cues are often an unconscious testing of boundaries. If left unchecked, they create a pattern of habitual overextension.

Once you become attuned to these signals, reclaiming control involves carefully redirecting the conversation about your workload and responsibilities. This begins by clarifying expectations at the outset and revisiting them regularly as projects evolve. When a new task arises, it's vital to pause and ask yourself how it fits within your existing commitments, what the deadlines are, and whether any adjustments to resources or priorities will accompany the additional work.

By posing these questions, you buy yourself much-needed time to evaluate your capacity and communicate a clear message that your availability isn't infinite. When it becomes clear that a task falls outside your agreed scope or would overload you, it's essential to articulate this honestly and professionally. You might explain that accommodating the new request would require adjusting other deadlines or reprioritizing work. You may frame your response in a way that invites collaboration, emphasizing your commitment to quality and the need to balance competing demands effectively.

Keeping a record of task requests and any agreements about your role and responsibilities is also a crucial practice. Not only does this protect you in the event of disputes, but it also provides a clear picture of when and how scope creep has occurred.

Transparency about your workload benefits everyone involved by setting realistic expectations.

Preventing scope creep is not about rigidly refusing any request but about exercising intentionality and ongoing communication. Advocating for your limits with confidence and without guilt is an essential form of professional stewardship. It preserves your ability to deliver excellent work sustainably and maintain your well-being.

As you strengthen your boundaries around workload and responsibilities, you'll find that colleagues and managers come to understand and respect your limits more clearly. Your role becomes focused and valued rather than diffuse and taken for granted. You move from being the default responder to everyone's extras to being a specialist who contributes strategically and sustainably.

In the next segment, we will explore how to approach those persistent last-minute requests that challenge your boundaries and learn to say no gracefully while maintaining professional relationships.

The Art of the Last-Minute No

There's a particular moment in the workday that many know too well, the moment just as you are about to wrap up, the moment your focus is at its peak or your energy is running low, when a seemingly small request lands in your inbox or someone appears at your desk with "just one more thing." These last-minute asks can feel urgent, necessary, and sometimes unavoidable. They carry an implicit expectation that you will drop everything and accommodate, that your generosity and flexibility will stretch to meet the immediate need without complaint.

Saying yes in these moments often seems like the easiest path. It's a way to maintain harmony, demonstrate your team spirit, or avoid the discomfort of refusal. But these "just one more thing" moments are where many professionals lose control of their time. They fracture the boundaries carefully built throughout the day and threaten to unravel the progress you've made toward balance.

To protect your professional and personal well-being, learning to navigate these last-minute requests with intention is crucial. The first step is to slow down, even briefly. Rather than reacting automatically, allow yourself a moment to breathe and assess. This pause shifts your response from reactive to deliberate. You start to consider whether you can take on the additional work without compromising quality or your mental health.

Sometimes, you may decide that saying yes is both possible and appropriate. When the task aligns with your priorities and you have the capacity, embracing flexibility can deepen collaboration and goodwill. But just as often, the answer will be no, or a qualified no that offers an alternative.

Expressing this kind of no gracefully involves acknowledging the urgency or importance of the request while communicating your limits. Instead of simply saying "I can't," you might say, "I understand this is important, but I'm currently focused on meeting a deadline that requires my full attention. I can look at this first thing tomorrow." This kind of response shows respect for the requester's needs and your boundaries simultaneously.

In situations where last-minute requests become a pattern, it may be necessary to broaden the conversation beyond the individual's request. You might find yourself discussing with your manager or team the need to establish clearer expectations around workflows and deadlines. Framing this dialogue positively, emphasizing your commitment to delivering quality work and avoiding burnout, helps ensure these conversations are constructive rather than confrontational.

One of the challenges in setting these boundaries is the fear of being perceived as inflexible or uncooperative. This is understandable, especially in cultures that prize hustle and immediate availability. However, setting limits around last-minute demands demonstrates professionalism and respect for your capacity, ultimately leading to more sustainable performance and greater respect from colleagues.

Over-apologizing when declining can unintentionally weaken your boundary. While kindness is essential, excessive apologies can make you seem needy or fragile. Instead, expressing appreciation for their understanding, such as "Thanks for understanding that I need to focus on my current priorities," asserts your limits with confidence.

Confidence in these moments often grows through practice. Role-playing or mentally rehearsing how you will respond to last-minute requests prepares you for the emotional challenge these situations can present. With time, responding to these interruptions with calm clarity becomes less daunting and more habitual.

The ability to say no to last-minute requests is not just a skill; it's an act of self-preservation. Protecting the boundaries around your time and energy preserves not only your effectiveness but your sense of balance and fulfillment in your work.

In the following segment, we will delve into the challenges and opportunities presented by remote work environments, where the boundaries between personal and professional life blur and the need for clear limits becomes even more pressing.

Drawing Lines in the Digital Space

The shift to remote work has transformed the way we experience professional boundaries. No longer confined by the walls of an office or the visible presence of colleagues, work now intrudes in subtle and persistent ways into the spaces where we eat, rest, and live. While remote work offers undeniable freedoms, it also blurs the lines between work time and personal time, creating a landscape where boundaries are both more necessary and more challenging to enforce.

Without the physical separation of a commute or an office environment, many find themselves tethered to screens for longer hours, their availability stretching beyond the traditional workday. The ping of emails and messages becomes a constant rhythm, and the expectation to respond promptly, regardless of the hour, intensifies. This "always-on" culture, while often unspoken, creates an invisible pressure to prioritize work above all else, eroding the restorative boundaries that protect mental health and prevent burnout.

In this context, defining and communicating clear boundaries is vital. It starts with clarifying your work hours, deciding when your professional day begins and ends, and committing to honoring those limits. This may mean turning off notifications outside of designated hours, setting your status to unavailable, or creating physical cues within your home that signal work time and personal time.

Communicating these boundaries to your team and clients is equally important. Letting others know your availability fosters mutual respect and sets realistic expectations. It's not about building walls but about creating a rhythm that sustains your productivity and wellbeing over time.

Yet, setting boundaries in remote work is not without its complexities. The virtual nature of communication can make refusals feel less personal and more prone to misunderstanding. Without face-to-face cues, a firm no can be interpreted as coldness or disengagement. Navigating this requires intentionality and empathy, pairing clear communication with warmth and presence, even in digital exchanges.

Remote work also demands discipline in managing task boundaries. The absence of structured office hours can lead to work creeping into evenings and weekends, often disguised as "catching up" or "preparing for the week ahead." Recognizing these habits is the first step to reclaiming your time.

Developing rituals to mark the start and end of your workday can be powerful. Whether it's a morning walk before logging on or a ritual of shutting down your computer and physically leaving your workspace, these acts signal to your brain and body the transition between professional and personal modes.

Moreover, remote work challenges us to be proactive in requesting support and negotiating workloads. Without informal office check-ins, it's easy to become isolated with mounting responsibilities. Setting regular check-ins with supervisors and colleagues creates space for dialogue about capacity and priorities, enabling boundaries to be respected collaboratively rather than imposed reactively.

Ultimately, the landscape of remote work requires a new kind of boundary literacy, one that embraces flexibility without sacrificing self-care and communication without surrendering clarity. It invites us to become architects of our professional rhythms, designing lives where work and rest coexist sustainably.

In the next segment, we will explore concrete communication strategies and scripts tailored to workplace boundaries, helping you to assert your limits with confidence, clarity, and kindness in a variety of professional scenarios.

Speaking Your Boundaries

Boundaries are only as effective as the clarity and intention behind how we communicate them. In professional settings, the challenge often lies not only in knowing where to draw the line but in expressing it in ways that maintain respect, trust, and connection. Speaking your boundaries confidently requires balancing firmness with empathy, honesty with diplomacy, and clarity with kindness.

Every workplace has its own culture, unwritten rules, and relational dynamics that shape how messages are received. The exact boundary can sound empowering in one environment and confrontational in another. Navigating this requires emotional intelligence, the ability to read the room, understand others' perspectives, and adjust your communication while holding to your core limits.

When preparing to express a boundary, begin by grounding yourself in your purpose. Remind yourself that your boundary serves your well-being and your capacity to contribute meaningfully. This mindset shifts the energy from defensive to declarative. You're not arguing or negotiating your worth; you're stating what is needed for sustainable engagement.

It helps to use "I" statements that focus on your experience rather than placing blame. For example, saying "I need to focus on current projects to maintain quality" centers your boundary in your needs instead of accusing others of unrealistic demands. This approach reduces defensiveness and invites understanding.

Equally important is pacing your delivery. Speak slowly and with a steady tone. Avoid trailing off or using uncertain language that undermines your position. Instead of "I guess I can try," say "I won't be able to take that on right now." This communicates resolve without aggression.

In situations where pushback is anticipated, pre-emptively acknowledging the other person's perspective can build rapport. For example, "I understand this is urgent, and I want to support the team, but I need to prioritize existing commitments." This shows empathy without sacrificing your limits.

Nonverbal cues also carry weight. Maintaining an open posture, making eye contact, and moderating your facial expressions signal confidence and openness, reinforcing your verbal message.

If a boundary requires negotiation, such as adjusting deadlines or redistributing tasks, approach the conversation collaboratively.

Frame your concerns in terms of shared goals: "To deliver the best results, I suggest we discuss reprioritizing some responsibilities." This positions you as solution-oriented rather than obstructive.

Remember, boundaries are dynamic. They may need revisiting as projects evolve and relationships shift. Regularly checking in with supervisors and colleagues about workload and expectations fosters ongoing alignment and prevents misunderstandings.

Mistakes and discomfort are part of the process. You may feel awkward or second-guess yourself initially. This is normal and doesn't reflect failure. Each time you express your boundaries, you build resilience and refine your communication skills.

Over time, speaking your boundaries with clarity and care reshapes how you are seen at work. You become known not just for your contributions but for your integrity and professionalism. Your limits inspire respect rather than resentment.

In the final segment of this chapter, we will examine real-life stories of professionals who transformed their careers by setting boundaries, offering inspiration, and providing practical wisdom for your journey.

Boundaries in Action

Boundaries at work are more than rules or limits; they are acts of courage that reshape careers, redefine relationships, and reclaim well-being. The stories of those who have learned to hold firm in professional spaces offer both inspiration and guidance for anyone ready to do the same.

Consider Maya, a project manager who had long been the go-to person for "just one more thing" requests. Early in her career, she said yes to nearly every task, driven by a desire to prove herself and maintain harmony. But the constant overcommitment led to exhaustion, missed deadlines, and simmering resentment. It wasn't until a particularly demanding quarter that Maya recognized she had to change. She began by tracking her workload, identifying where scope creep had taken root. Then she started saying no, not abruptly or harshly, but with calm clarity. "I'm focusing on these key deliverables right now," she would say, "and need to prioritize accordingly." Over time, Maya's colleagues adjusted to her new boundaries, and her work quality and job satisfaction soared. She became known not just for her reliability but for her integrity and leadership.

Then there's Carlos, a remote software developer who struggled with the blurred lines of work and home life. Without clear limits, he found himself responding to messages late into the night and on weekends, slowly burning out. Carlos decided to carve out strict work hours and communicated them openly to his team. He set his status to "offline" outside those hours and resisted the urge to check email compulsively. When last-minute requests came, he responded with gratitude but firmness, explaining when he could realistically address the issue. His team initially pushed back, but they soon came to respect Carlos's approach as it improved his focus and output. Carlos reclaimed his evenings and weekends, strengthening his relationships and renewing his passion for his work.

Another story comes from Aisha, a client relations specialist who often faced emotional labor beyond her job description.

Clients expected her to be endlessly available and emotionally supportive, which drained her energy. Recognizing this pattern, Aisha began setting clear boundaries around her availability and the scope of her support. She crafted scripts to gently but firmly redirect conversations and set expectations. Over time, Aisha noticed a shift: clients respected her limits, and her stress decreased. She found more space for professional growth and personal joy.

These stories share common threads: the recognition that boundaries are necessary; the willingness to communicate them clearly; the patience to face initial resistance; and the persistence to maintain limits over time. They remind us that boundaries are not fixed walls but living practices that evolve with our careers and lives.

Boundaries at work may feel risky at first, but they are investments in your sustainability and success. They protect your time and energy, enhance your credibility, and deepen respect in your professional relationships. By embracing boundaries, you don't just survive work; you thrive in it.

As this chapter closes, carry forward the understanding that your professional worth is not measured by how many tasks you accept but by the quality and authenticity of your contributions. Your boundaries are the foundation on which your worth stands firm.

In the next chapter, we'll shift focus to boundaries within personal relationships, the messy, beautiful, complex terrain where emotions run deep and stakes feel even higher.

While professional boundaries carry their complexities, the personal realm often presents even greater emotional challenges.

Relationships with friends, family, and partners test our boundaries in deeply intimate ways. The next chapter explores how to navigate these emotional landscapes with courage and care.

Chapter 8: The Heart's Borders

Why Boundaries in Relationships Matter

Personal relationships are where our boundaries are most deeply tested, stretched, and sometimes shattered. They are also the places where the stakes feel highest, the arenas where love, loyalty, history, and hope entwine in complex ways. Unlike professional settings, where roles and expectations can be more defined and transactional, relationships are layered with emotional nuance, unspoken agreements, and long histories that shape how boundaries are understood and respected or ignored.

Setting boundaries with friends, family, and partners is an act that often evokes guilt, fear, and uncertainty. The voices from childhood and culture whisper that family ties are unconditional, that friendship means sacrifice, that love requires endless giving. Yet, these very expectations can become cages if boundaries are absent. Without clear limits, personal connections risk becoming sites of emotional exhaustion, resentment, and even harm.

Imagine the scenario of a sibling who constantly relies on you to manage family drama or absorb emotional burdens, yet offers little support in return. Or a partner whose needs consistently overshadow yours, leaving you depleted. Or a friend who expects your availability without regard for your own life's demands. These patterns can erode your sense of self and diminish the joy that relationships are meant to bring.

Boundaries in relationships aren't about shutting others out or withholding love. They aim to create a space where connection can be authentic, sustainable, and mutually nourishing. They ensure that you show up as your whole self rather than as a fragmented version depleted by obligation and overextension.

At the heart of relational boundaries is the recognition that you cannot give what you do not have. Your capacity to love, listen, and be present depends on how well you protect your energy and respect your needs. Without boundaries, love can become an endless well that dries up, leaving both parties parched.

Yet, boundaries in personal relationships are complicated by emotions. Saying no to a friend or family member can feel like betrayal. The histories embedded in these bonds make asserting limits fraught with risk, risk of disappointment, conflict, or even rejection. This risk is real and must be acknowledged. But so too is the cost of silence: a slow erosion of self that can leave you bitter, resentful, or disengaged.

Understanding boundaries in relationships requires a shift from seeing them as barriers to seeing them as bridges, bridges that connect you more honestly to others and yourself. They are invitations to more profound respect, more transparent communication, and more balanced exchanges. When boundaries are in place, love is not about sacrifice alone but about reciprocity.

This chapter will navigate the unique terrain of personal boundaries. We will explore common relational traps, such as the "but we're family" argument, guilt loops, and enmeshment that blur the lines between you and others. We'll explore how to set boundaries without pushing others away, and when distance is a necessary act of self-preservation.

We'll also consider the emotional labor often invisible in relationships, those unseen efforts that disproportionately fall on some people, usually women, and how boundaries can protect against this exhaustion. Scripts and scenarios will help you find your voice in emotionally charged conversations, from holiday negotiations to managing financial boundaries with loved ones.

Ultimately, this chapter invites you to reclaim your relational energy with courage and compassion. To show up more fully in your connections, not less. To love not from depletion, but from a place of wholeness.

The work is not easy. Boundaries in relationships are messy, fluid, and deeply personal. But they are also transformative. When you set them clearly and lovingly, you give yourself permission to exist fully and invite others to do the same.

In the next segment, we'll begin by unpacking the common relational patterns that undermine boundaries and how to recognize when you're caught in them.

Tangled Threads, Recognizing Patterns

In the intricate web of personal relationships, specific patterns repeatedly emerge, quietly eroding boundaries and trapping individuals in cycles of over-giving, resentment, and exhaustion. These relational patterns often go unnoticed at first, appearing as acts of love or duty, only to reveal themselves over time as emotional drain or obligation.

One such pattern is the unspoken expectation that family means unconditional availability. This belief, deeply ingrained in many cultures and families, suggests that saying no to a relative is

THE BOOK ON SAYING NO

tantamount to betrayal. The phrase "But we're family" becomes a verbal leash, tethering people to duties they may not want or have the capacity for. This often leads to individuals sacrificing their needs to preserve peace or uphold tradition, despite internal resistance.

Similarly, enmeshment can blur the boundaries between individuals, creating relationships where personal identities and needs become entangled. In these dynamics, one person's emotions, decisions, or behaviors feel inseparable from the other's. It becomes difficult to discern where one ends and the other begins, asserting boundaries fraught with guilt and confusion. Enmeshment often manifests as a subtle pressure to comply or to prioritize the relationship's harmony over individual well-being.

Another common relational trap is the cycle of guilt loops. Here, saying no triggers feelings of guilt that lead to over-explanation, apology, or eventual compliance. The person setting the boundary may find themselves caught in a loop of self-justification, trying to soften the impact of their refusal in hopes of preserving the relationship. This cycle undermines the boundary's effectiveness and reinforces the belief that their needs are less important.

These patterns can be especially challenging in friendships and partnerships, where emotional history and mutual vulnerability heighten sensitivity to rejection. People often fear that asserting limits will lead to abandonment or judgment, so they remain silent or acquiesce, even at personal cost.

Recognizing these patterns requires honest self-reflection and sometimes an external perspective. Ask yourself: Do I feel pressured to say yes because of who is asking? Do I hesitate or apologize excessively when expressing a boundary? Do I feel responsible for others' emotions or reactions? Do I struggle to separate my needs from theirs?

Awareness is the first step to untangling these threads. Once you can name the patterns, you can begin to disrupt them with intention. Boundaries become not walls but clarifying lines that honor both connection and individuality.

It's important to remember that breaking these cycles is not a one-time event but a process. It involves experimenting with new ways of relating, practicing saying no without guilt, and learning to tolerate the discomfort that comes with change. Support from trusted friends, mentors, or therapists can be invaluable in navigating this terrain.

As you move forward, keep in mind that healthy relationships do not demand your silence or sacrifice. They evolve with honesty and mutual respect. Boundaries are the scaffolding that supports this evolution, allowing relationships to breathe, grow, and deepen authentically.

In the next segment, we will explore practical strategies for holding boundaries in emotionally charged situations, including conversations with family members and partners where stakes feel particularly high.

Holding Space, Navigating Boundaries

When boundaries arise in personal relationships, the conversations that follow often carry an emotional weight unlike many other areas of life. With family, friends, or partners, saying no can feel like opening a door to disappointment, frustration, or even conflict. This emotional intensity can make it challenging to hold boundaries with both firmness and compassion.

One of the first challenges is managing the impulse to soften or withdraw to protect the relationship. The desire to avoid tension is natural; none of us wants to hurt those we love or risk rejection. Yet, over-softening a boundary often dilutes its clarity and effectiveness, leaving both parties confused and needs unmet.

To navigate these moments, it's vital to hold space for emotions, both yours and theirs, without sacrificing your limits. Holding space means acknowledging feelings without becoming overwhelmed by them or taking responsibility for them. It means listening with empathy, while remaining anchored in your truth.

For example, if a family member reacts with hurt or anger when you set a boundary, you can say, "I hear that this is difficult for you, and I want you to know my intention isn't to push you away, but to take care of myself." This response validates their feelings without retreating from your boundary.

It's also helpful to anticipate common emotional reactions and prepare yourself emotionally. You may feel anxiety, guilt, or sadness, and that's normal. Recognize these feelings as part of the process, not signs you've made a mistake. Your emotional experience is valid, but it doesn't negate your right to boundaries.

Another key aspect is clear and calm communication. Speak your needs in simple, direct language. Avoid blaming or accusing, which can escalate tensions. Instead, focus on your experience and needs, using "I" statements: "I need time to recharge," or "I'm not able to take this on right now."

Body language plays a decisive role. Maintaining open posture, steady eye contact, and a calm tone helps convey sincerity and confidence. It also helps regulate your nervous system, reducing the chances of being swept into emotional reactivity.

Sometimes, despite your best efforts, conversations become heated or unproductive. In such cases, it's okay to pause the discussion and revisit it later when emotions have settled. Saying, "I want to talk about this more when we're both feeling calmer," honors both your boundary and the relationship.

Boundary-setting in emotionally charged relationships is rarely a one-time event. It's a process of repeated affirmation, testing, and recalibration. With patience and persistence, it's possible to establish a new rhythm of respect and understanding.

In the following segment, we will delve into specific scripts and approaches for everyday boundary conversations, holidays, money, and emotional labor that readers can adapt to their own lives.

Conversations That Matter

Specific conversations in personal relationships carry a unique weight, especially those involving holidays, finances, and emotional labor. These topics often surface deeply rooted expectations and unspoken assumptions, making boundary-setting feel especially daunting. Yet, these are precisely the moments when clear, compassionate communication is most needed.

Take holidays, for example. These times, loaded with tradition and expectation, can become pressure cookers. Invitations to attend every event, perform endless tasks, or manage family dynamics may feel less like choices and more like obligations. It's common to fear that saying no, or even expressing limits, might spark disappointment or familial tension.

Navigating holiday boundaries begins with recognizing that your well-being matters. You don't need to participate in every gathering or fulfill every role, no matter what has been expected historically. Articulating this gently but firmly can be transformative. You might say, "I love our family traditions, and this year I'm choosing to rest and celebrate in a smaller way. I hope you understand." This frames your decision as one of self-care rather than rejection.

Money is another complex boundary terrain. Financial requests or expectations from family or friends can entangle relationships in a delicate balance of generosity, obligation, and power. Saying no to lending money or participating in shared expenses may feel uncomfortable or guilt-inducing, especially when relationships are close or longstanding.

Clarity around financial boundaries involves honesty about your limits and values. You might say, "I'm not able to lend money right now, but I want to support you in other ways," or "I prefer to keep our finances separate so that our relationship stays strong." Such statements set limits while affirming care.

Emotional labor, the unseen work of managing feelings, smoothing tensions, and offering support, is often disproportionately shouldered by some individuals, leaving them drained. Setting boundaries here requires naming this labor and communicating your limits. For example, "I want to be there for you, but I need to protect my energy. I may not always be available to process everything right away." This asserts your needs while maintaining connection.

In all these conversations, it's essential to prepare for resistance. People may express hurt, confusion, or disappointment. Holding your boundary means listening without over-explaining or capitulating. You can acknowledge their feelings while reaffirming your limits: "I understand this feels difficult, and I hope we can find ways to support each other within these boundaries."

These scripts are not rigid formulas but starting points. Your voice, tone, and context will shape their delivery. Practicing them aloud, imagining the conversation, and tuning into your feelings can help build confidence.

Ultimately, these conversations invite a new kind of relational honesty, one where your needs are visible and valued, and relationships grow not despite boundaries, but because of them.

In the next segment, we'll explore self-assessment tools to help you identify where your relational energy leaks most, so you can focus your boundary work where it matters most deeply.

Where Your Energy Goes

Personal relationships, for all their richness, can be a source of both profound nourishment and subtle depletion. The emotional currency you invest —time, attention, empathy, and availability —can either be returned in balance or quietly drained, leaving you feeling empty, exhausted, and disconnected from your own needs.

Understanding where your relational energy leaks most is a crucial step in boundary work. Often, we enter relationships carrying assumptions about what we must give, which can obscure the realities of how that giving impacts us. You might find yourself repeatedly drained by certain people or patterns without fully realizing the cumulative toll.

A reflective self-assessment invites you to slow down and consider which relationships or dynamics feel most taxing. Do specific family gatherings leave you emotionally exhausted? Does one-sided support characterize a particular friendship? Do you notice yourself saying yes out of guilt rather than desire?

Notice not only what drains you but also what nourishes you. Relationships that replenish your spirit tend to honor your boundaries naturally, offering reciprocity and respect. Those that leave you depleted often coincide with blurred limits, unspoken expectations, or emotional enmeshment.

This assessment isn't a judgment but an invitation to clarity. It helps you pinpoint where boundary-setting will have the most significant impact, not in a reactive or punitive way, but as a form of self-care that ultimately enhances the quality of your connections.

Consider creating a simple mental map or journal entry, noting interactions or people that leave you feeling energized versus drained. Over time, patterns emerge. You may discover that specific relational roles, such as caretaker, mediator, or confidante, are more exhausting than others, or that particular topics or contexts repeatedly trigger overwhelm.

Armed with this awareness, you can begin to experiment with setting limits selectively and intentionally. Perhaps it means declining certain invitations, limiting the time you spend with draining individuals, or clarifying what support you are willing and able to provide.

Reclaiming your power in relationships also means acknowledging your right to prioritize yourself without guilt. This shift often challenges deeply internalized beliefs about obligation and loyalty but is essential for sustaining authentic connection.

As you practice these boundaries, notice how your emotional landscape changes. You may initially experience discomfort or resistance, both from within and from others, as dynamics shift. This is natural and part of the growth process.

Yet, with persistence, boundaries become a source of freedom. They clarify who you are, what you value, and how you want to show up. They invite others to meet you with respect and presence, fostering deeper, more balanced connections.

In the following segment, we will begin to explore the intimate territory of romantic partnerships and how boundaries can support love that is both connected and autonomous.

Love and Limits

Romantic relationships are often the most profound and vulnerable arenas for boundary-setting. In love, the intertwining of two lives invites closeness and connection unlike any other, but it also demands the courage to maintain individuality and self-respect amid intimacy.

Many enter partnerships with the hope of union and acceptance, yet the dance of closeness can quickly blur personal boundaries. It's common to lose sight of where you end and your partner begins, especially when emotional needs are intense and histories complex. This enmeshment can lead to sacrificing your desires or tolerating discomfort to avoid conflict or rejection.

Healthy boundaries in romantic relationships are the foundation for a love that nurtures both connection and autonomy. They allow each partner to show up fully and honestly, free from the pressures of codependence or obligation.

Setting these boundaries begins with self-awareness, knowing your values, needs, and limits, and the willingness to express them with kindness and clarity. It might look like communicating your need for alone time, setting expectations around communication styles, or discussing financial boundaries openly.

Challenges inevitably arise. Fear of hurting the other, guilt about seeming "selfish," or anxiety about upsetting the relationship can make boundary-setting feel risky. But silence and compliance come at a cost: diminished selfhood, growing resentment, and emotional fatigue.

Navigating this terrain requires ongoing dialogue and mutual respect. Boundaries are not rigid walls but flexible guidelines that evolve as partners grow individually and together. They invite honesty, foster trust, and create space for healing old wounds that can complicate intimacy.

In moments of tension, it helps to approach conversations from a place of shared care rather than blame. Express your needs using "I" statements and invite your partner's perspective with openness. For example, "I feel overwhelmed when plans change at the last minute. Can we find a way to communicate changes earlier?" This models respect and invites collaboration.

Partners may react defensively or with confusion initially, which is normal. Patience and consistency are key. Over time, as boundaries are maintained with compassion, they strengthen the relationship's foundation rather than erode it.

Ultimately, boundaries in romantic partnerships are acts of love, not just for the other but for yourself. They honor your worth and invite your partner to love you as a whole, autonomous being.

As this chapter draws to a close, reflect on how boundaries in your closest relationships can transform connection from survival to thriving. The next chapter will turn inward, exploring the critical frontier of setting boundaries with yourself, the inner yes and no that shapes every other choice.

Chapter 9: The Inner Dialogue

Understanding the Boundaries

The relationship you have with yourself is the most intimate and enduring of all. Before you can say no to others, you must learn to say no within your mind, to the internal impulses, habits, and beliefs that shape your behavior. Inner boundaries govern how you manage your energy, your attention, and ultimately, the direction of your life.

Many people live with a constant internal struggle between desire and discipline, between what feels good in the moment and what serves them in the long run. This tension is a fundamental aspect of being human, but it can become a source of distress when inner boundaries are weak or absent.

Consider the impulses that often override your best intentions: the urge to overcommit, to overwork, to over-plan. The drive to please, to avoid discomfort, or to seek external validation can lead you to say yes to activities and demands that do not align with your true priorities.

Perfectionism and toxic productivity are often at the heart of this internal struggle. The voice that tells you "You must do more," "You should be better," or "You can't rest until this is perfect" is a boundary breaker. It dismisses your need for rest, your limits, and your humanity.

Emotional boundaries with your inner critic, the relentless commentator inside your head, are essential. Learning to recognize when this voice is serving you, and when it is

SAGE MONROE

sabotaging you, is the first step toward reclaiming your internal landscape.

Setting internal boundaries involves tuning into your body's signals and feelings, distinguishing between gut wisdom and guilt-driven urges. It means honoring when you need rest rather than pushing through exhaustion, choosing quality over quantity, and accepting that "good enough" often is.

Time-blocking and creating non-negotiable rest periods are practical tools that support inner boundaries. They help you say no to the tyranny of urgency and yes to sustainable rhythms.

An empowering practice in this domain is the "reverse to-do list," where you intentionally note what you will no longer do, what you are committed to dropping or avoiding, freeing yourself from the shackles of endless obligation.

The inner yes and no shape every external choice. Strengthening these boundaries cultivates self-respect, reduces burnout, and lays the groundwork for a life aligned with your deepest values.

In the next segment, we will explore practical methods for identifying and strengthening these internal limits, and how to distinguish when your inner voice is guiding you toward growth versus when it is enforcing harmful patterns.

Listening Within

Our inner landscape is a complex interplay of voices, impulses, and sensations. Some guide us toward authentic growth, rest, and alignment. Others pull us into cycles of self-judgment, exhaustion, and disconnection. Learning to distinguish

163

between these inner signals is fundamental to building healthy internal boundaries.

Gut wisdom arises from a place of embodied knowing, a deep, intuitive sense of what serves your wellbeing. It is often subtle yet persistent, manifesting as a quiet feeling of alignment or discomfort. When you listen with openness and curiosity, this inner guidance can become a trustworthy compass.

In contrast, guilt's whisper is a learned response, an echo of external expectations and internalized "shoulds." It can feel urgent and loud, urging you to act out of obligation or fear rather than desire or necessity. Guilt often triggers tension in the body, characterized by a tightening in the chest, a knot in the stomach, and a clouding of clarity.

Distinguishing these feelings requires cultivating self-awareness and patience. It means slowing down enough to notice how your body responds to different choices and to what motivations are driving your actions.

For example, you may feel an intuitive pull to rest after a long day, your body's way of signaling a needed boundary. But guilt may push you to keep working, insisting that your value depends on productivity. When you tune in, you notice the difference between a gentle invitation to pause and a harsh internal command to perform.

Practices such as mindfulness, journaling, and body scans can enhance this listening. They help you observe your thoughts and sensations without judgment, creating space for clarity to emerge.

Setting boundaries with your inner critic also involves challenging the stories it tells. When it says, "You're lazy if you don't finish this," or "You don't deserve rest," pause and ask whether this is the truth or fear. Reframe these narratives to ones that honor your humanity: "I am enough as I am," or "Rest fuels my creativity and health."

Strengthening these internal limits empowers you to choose actions aligned with your values rather than reactive patterns. It supports saying no to overcommitment and yes to sustainable rhythms.

In the next segment, we will explore practical strategies for time management and self-care that embody these internal boundaries, helping you translate inner clarity into daily practice.

Creating Sacred Time

The dance between your inner yes and no finds its clearest expression in how you manage your time, the most finite resource you have. Time-blocking, the deliberate allocation of specific periods for work, rest, and self-care, transforms the abstract concept of boundaries into concrete practice. It is a powerful tool for honoring your internal limits and reclaiming agency over your day.

By setting aside blocks of time dedicated to focused work, you prevent distractions and create a container that supports productivity without overwhelm. Equally important are the blocks reserved for rest, those sacred pauses where your body and mind replenish and your nervous system resets.

Non-negotiable rest periods might seem radical in a culture that glorifies busyness and productivity, but they are essential. Without them, your energy dissipates like water through a sieve, and no matter how much you accomplish, exhaustion looms.

Practicing these boundaries requires commitment and compassion. The first step is to observe your current patterns. When do you feel most energized? When do you notice fatigue creeping in? Mapping these rhythms helps you design a schedule that works with your body, not against it.

Once you identify these natural cycles, you can begin to block time intentionally. For example, mornings might be devoted to deep work when focus is highest, while afternoons include time for meetings or lighter tasks. Crucially, rest periods, whether brief breaks or longer pauses, are scheduled and honored as firmly as any appointment.

Building this structure invites a gentle but firm no to reactive distractions and overextension. It says, "This time is reserved for me," creating a sanctuary within your day.

Another practice is the creation of a "reverse to-do list," a conscious acknowledgment of tasks and commitments you will intentionally let go. This practice relieves the weight of endless obligation and clarifies your priorities.

Through these methods, you cultivate self-respect and trust, trust that your needs matter, that rest is not weakness, and that boundaries are a form of radical self-love.

In the next segment, we will explore the critical role of your inner critic and how to establish emotional boundaries with this relentless inner voice.

Taming the Inner Critic, Setting Emotional Boundaries Within

The inner critic is a familiar companion for many, a relentless voice that questions, judges, and diminishes. This internal commentator often masquerades as motivation or self-protection, but its unyielding presence can sabotage your confidence, erode self-esteem, and undermine your boundaries, both internal and external.

Recognizing the inner critic as a separate entity is the first step toward establishing emotional boundaries with it. Rather than identifying with its harsh messages, you learn to observe its words with curiosity and compassion. It is not your truth, but a learned script shaped by past experiences, cultural messages, and unmet needs.

Setting emotional boundaries with the inner critic involves refusing to give it unchecked power over your decisions and self-worth. When it says, "You're not good enough," or "You don't deserve rest," you practice naming these statements as falsehoods rather than facts. This process requires patience; the critic's voice may resist, growing louder or more persistent when challenged.

Mindfulness practices offer powerful tools here. By cultivating awareness of your thoughts and feelings without immediate reaction, you create space to respond rather than react. You learn to recognize when the critic is speaking and choose whether to engage or gently redirect your attention.

Another practical approach is to develop a compassionate inner dialogue, a counter voice that affirms your worth and supports your boundaries. This might sound like, "I am doing my best, and that is enough," or "Taking care of myself allows me to show up fully."

Journaling can also be a helpful practice, giving form to your inner experiences and allowing you to explore the origins of your critical voice. Understanding its roots can diminish its power.

Establishing these emotional boundaries strengthens your capacity to hold external boundaries. When your inner world is kinder and more supportive, you stand firmer in saying no to others without internal sabotage.

In the next segment, we will focus on building a "reverse to-do list" as a tool to concretize these internal boundaries and reclaim your time and energy.

The Power of Saying No to Tasks

In a world that celebrates productivity and accumulation, the act of consciously deciding what you will no longer do is a radical form of boundary-setting. The reverse to-do list invites you to shift perspective, not only focusing on what needs to be done but intentionally declaring what you are removing from your plate.

This practice can feel liberating. It gives form to your limits and tangibly clarifies your priorities. By naming the tasks, commitments, or roles you will release, you make space for what truly matters, whether that be rest, creativity, connection, or deeper work.

Creating a reverse to-do list requires honesty and courage. It asks you to confront the habits, obligations, and expectations that no longer serve you, even if they come from external pressures or internalized "shoulds." It might include saying no to volunteer roles, to social events that drain you, to perfectionistic standards that sap your energy.

The list becomes a living document, evolving as you grow and your needs shift. Each item removed is a reclaiming of your time, energy, and self-respect.

Sharing your reverse to-do list with trusted friends or mentors can provide accountability and support, helping you hold to these new limits in the face of potential pushback.

Over time, this practice cultivates a mindset that values subtraction as much as addition. It reminds you that boundaries are not just about refusal but about intentional presence, choosing where to invest your precious resources with awareness and love.

In the next chapter, we will expand on this foundation, exploring how to align your yeses with your core values and vision, creating a life guided by purpose and intentionality.

Having begun to master the internal dialogue and self-discipline required to say no to yourself, the journey continues into an empowering place: saying yes intentionally. Chapter 10 guides you to align your yeses with your deepest values and visions, creating a life that is both purposeful and fulfilling.

Chapter 10: Saying Yes to What Matters

Aligning Your Commitments with Your Core Values

In the journey of reclaiming your time and boundaries, learning to say no is only part of the story. Equally transformative is learning to say yes, not indiscriminately, but deliberately and in alignment with what truly matters to you. Saying yes with intention is the art of prioritizing your highest values, passions, and long-term vision, creating a life infused with purpose rather than overwhelm.

True yeses feel embodied; they resonate deeply in your body and mind. They bring a sense of alignment and enthusiasm rather than obligation or guilt. When you say yes to what matters, your commitments become extensions of who you are, not distractions from who you want to be.

Identifying these core values is foundational. Values act as a compass, guiding decisions large and small. They might include creativity, connection, learning, health, freedom, or integrity. Reflecting on moments when you felt most fulfilled or proud can illuminate these priorities.

Once clarified, you can use your values as a filter through which all invitations and demands pass. This filter asks, "Does this support my values and vision?" If not, it's an invitation to say no, freeing space for what aligns.

Aligning your yeses also means redesigning your calendar and commitments to reflect these priorities. It's an intentional curation of your time and energy, ensuring that your daily actions weave into the tapestry of your desired life.

This alignment invites a shift from reactive to proactive living. Rather than responding to external pressures, you cultivate a habit of choosing commitments that nourish your goals and well-being.

In this process, it's vital to cultivate awareness of how different yeses feel. A yes that drains or distracts signals a misalignment, while a yes that energizes and fulfills confirms you're on track.

This chapter will guide you through exercises to uncover your highest ROI (return on investment), those commitments and activities that yield the most excellent personal and professional satisfaction and growth.

As you deepen this practice, you'll notice a growing sense of freedom and clarity. Boundaries cease to feel restrictive and instead become enablers of a meaningful, vibrant life.

In the next segment, we will explore how to create your list of highest ROI yeses and begin reshaping your commitments around them.

Prioritizing What Truly Counts

To say yes to what truly matters, you first need clarity on what those things are. This clarity comes from reflecting deeply on your life's activities, relationships, and goals to identify the commitments that provide the greatest return on your investment, your time, energy, and passion.

Return on investment, or ROI, in this context means more than just financial gain. It encompasses emotional satisfaction, personal growth, alignment with your values, and contributions to your overall life vision. High ROI yeses are those that energize you, move you forward, and foster meaningful connection or achievement.

Start by examining your current commitments. What activities or roles leave you feeling fulfilled and invigorated? Which ones drain your energy or feel like distractions? What patterns emerge when you reflect on when you've felt most alive or proud in your work or personal life?

Next, consider your long-term goals and values. Are your yeses aligned with these? For example, if creativity is a core value, do your commitments provide space for expression? If family connection is central, does your schedule reflect that priority?

Creating a personal list of highest ROI yeses involves prioritizing these activities and relationships explicitly. This list becomes a tool for decision-making, a benchmark against which to measure new opportunities.

This process also involves recognizing the cost of your yeses. Every yes is a no to something else, whether it's time for rest, relationships, or other passions. Embracing this trade-off is crucial to living intentionally rather than reactively.

With your list in hand, begin reshaping your calendar and commitments around it. This may mean declining invitations, delegating tasks, or restructuring your daily routines to protect time for these priorities.

As you make these shifts, observe how your energy and satisfaction change. You may find a renewed sense of purpose and flow, as your yeses reinforce rather than deplete you.

This practice is not static; your highest ROI yeses will evolve as you grow, and your circumstances change. Regular reflection ensures your commitments remain aligned with your values and vision.

In the next segment, we will explore techniques for maintaining this alignment over time, especially in the face of external pressures and shifting priorities.

Maintaining Alignment Amid External Pressures

Once you have identified your highest ROI yeses and begun reshaping your life around them, the ongoing challenge is maintaining that alignment when outside forces pull you in conflicting directions. Life is dynamic, and priorities shift, but the commitment to your core values can serve as an anchor during turbulent moments.

External pressures often come cloaked as opportunities, obligations, or urgent requests. The temptation to say yes, to avoid conflict, to seize every chance, or to fulfill perceived expectations, is strong. These moments test your resolve and the boundaries you have worked hard to establish.

Maintaining alignment requires vigilance and self-compassion. It's essential to check in with yourself regularly: Are my current commitments still serving my values? Am I feeling energized or depleted? What adjustments are needed to stay on course?

Developing rituals of reflection, such as weekly reviews, journaling, or mindfulness practices, can help you track these shifts and recalibrate as needed. These practices deepen self-awareness and reinforce your intention to live deliberately.

Equally vital is the ability to communicate your evolving boundaries with clarity and grace. As your priorities change, relationships and commitments may need renegotiation. This can feel uncomfortable, but honesty fosters respect and prevents resentment.

When faced with new requests or opportunities, applying your values-based filter prevents reactive decision-making. Ask yourself: Does this contribute meaningfully to my highest priorities, or does it dilute my focus?

Learning to say no with confidence in these moments strengthens your boundaries and reinforces your alignment. It also models for others the importance of intentional living.

Remember, maintaining alignment is a journey rather than a destination. It involves flexibility, patience, and the willingness to let go of what no longer fits. Each time you choose a yes rooted in your values, you build momentum toward a life of purpose and fulfillment.

In the next segment, we will explore how to integrate these practices into your daily routines and long-term planning, making aligned living a sustainable habit.

Embedding Alignment

Living in alignment with your core values isn't a fleeting project; it's a lifestyle, a daily commitment that shapes every choice you make. The process of embedding your highest ROI yeses into the fabric of your life requires intentional habits and thoughtful planning that honor both your immediate needs and your long-term vision.

Start by creating daily rituals that reflect your priorities, whether it's dedicating morning moments to creative work, carving out time for meaningful connection, or setting aside space for rest and rejuvenation. These rituals act as anchors, bringing your values from abstract ideas into lived experience.

Planning is equally vital. Long-term goals often feel distant and overwhelming, but breaking them down into manageable steps and aligning your weekly or monthly tasks with these goals keeps your path clear. When your daily actions resonate with your values, motivation flows naturally, and distractions lose their power.

Flexibility remains key. Life's unpredictability means that your priorities will shift, sometimes unexpectedly. By regularly revisiting and revising your plans, you stay connected to your evolving self. This ongoing dialogue with yourself nurtures growth and prevents stagnation.

Accountability structures, whether through trusted friends, mentors, or journaling, support your commitment. Sharing your intentions and progress invites encouragement and gentle course correction when needed.

Most importantly, embrace the messiness of this journey. Alignment is not perfection. There will be days when you stray, succumb to old habits, or face unforeseen demands. These moments offer learning, not failure. Each choice to realign is a victory, a reaffirmation of your commitment to yourself.

In this way, boundaries and alignment become partners. Boundaries protect the space where your values can flourish, while alignment infuses your boundaries with meaning and direction.

As you weave these practices into your life, you craft a story where your yeses are not scattered compromises but deliberate, powerful affirmations of who you are and who you are becoming.

In the next chapter, we will explore the transformational potential of saying no, illustrating how one empowered refusal can ripple outward to reshape identity, relationships, and life trajectory.

Chapter 11: The Ripple Begins

How One No Can Change Everything

The power of a single no is often underestimated. At first glance, a no may seem like a small act, a brief word uttered in a moment of discomfort or hesitation. But beneath its surface lies a transformative force, one capable of reshaping identity, relationships, and even the trajectory of a life.

Saying no is a boundary, yes, but it is also a declaration of self. When you say no, you claim your own time, energy, and priorities. You communicate that your needs matter as much as others', that your life is worthy of respect and care. This assertion reverberates far beyond the immediate moment, challenging old patterns of compliance and people-pleasing that may have dominated for years.

The ripple effect of a no can be subtle or immediate, depending on context. For some, it triggers a newfound sense of freedom, a lightness borne from refusing to carry burdens not theirs to bear. For others, it sparks tension in relationships accustomed to habitual yeses, forcing a renegotiation of dynamics long taken for granted.

Consider Anna, a woman who had spent decades saying yes to every request from family, friends, and colleagues. When she first began saying no, it was terrifying. She feared backlash and loss. Yet, with each refusal, she felt more herself, clearer, stronger, and more grounded. Over time, her relationships shifted. Some grew deeper, now based on honesty rather than obligation. Others faded, revealing which connections had thrived on her acquiescence rather than a genuine connection.

Anna's story illustrates a truth many discover that no is not a rejection but a recalibration. It redefines how you relate to others and how they relate to you. Saying no can reveal who respects your boundaries, and who does not.

It also invites internal transformation. The act of saying no rewires neural pathways, reinforcing self-respect and reducing the internal anxiety associated with boundary-setting. This neurological shift supports greater ease in future refusals, creating a positive feedback loop that strengthens autonomy.

Yet, this transformation is not always linear or comfortable. The first no may feel like a rupture, shaking identity and relationships alike. Doubt, guilt, and fear often accompany the initial steps, challenging resolve. But these feelings are signs of growth, not failure.

Saying no disrupts the status quo. It challenges the invisible contracts we hold, contracts that demand sacrifice, silence, or invisibility in exchange for belonging or approval. Breaking these contracts awakens a new narrative, one where your life is yours to shape.

The ripple of a single no can extend into new realms: career changes, shifts in social circles, or a reimagining of personal goals. It is a catalyst for pivoting toward authenticity and alignment.

As this chapter unfolds, we will explore stories like Anna's and others who harnessed the power of no to enact profound change. We will explore how a single refusal can lead to healing burnout, mending strained relationships, or paving new paths.

In the next segment, we will delve deeper into the internal shifts that accompany this transformation, the emotional and psychological changes that allow one to become not just a word, but a way of life.

The Inner Shift: Embracing the Emotional Transformation

Saying no is more than a verbal act; it is an invitation to profound inner transformation. Beneath the surface of each refusal lies a reorientation of how you view yourself and your place in the world. This shift is often subtle but powerfully liberating, reshaping your relationship with fear, guilt, and self-worth.

At the beginning of this journey, many people feel they're not at risk. There is a tension between wanting to assert their needs and the fear of losing connection, approval, or love. This tension manifests as emotional resistance, anxiety, guilt, shame, or self-doubt, which can make boundary-setting feel like walking on a tightrope.

However, with each act of saying no, these fears begin to lose their grip. You start to see that discomfort does not equate to danger and that disappointing others is not synonymous with betrayal. This realization rewires your emotional responses, allowing you to hold your boundaries with increasing calm and confidence.

This internal shift is a form of healing. It restores the integrity of your self-image, aligning your actions with your actual values rather than external pressures. It reduces the cognitive dissonance that comes from living out of sync with yourself, replacing it with coherence and peace.

Psychologically, this shift also strengthens your locus of control, the belief that you have agency over your life. By saying no, you reclaim decision-making power, moving from reactive compliance to proactive choice. This empowerment spills over into other areas, fostering resilience and autonomy.

Emotionally, you cultivate greater self-compassion. You learn to treat yourself with the same kindness you offer others, understanding that setting limits is an act of love, not selfishness. This nurturance builds a foundation of inner safety, reducing the need to seek validation externally.

Physiologically, the nervous system responds to this transformation. Practices of boundary-setting activate the parasympathetic nervous system, the branch responsible for rest and restoration, helping to soothe chronic stress responses associated with people-pleasing and overcommitment.

As these shifts deepen, no evolves from a momentary act into a habit and eventually a value, a guiding principle for living authentically. You begin to experience your boundaries as extensions of your self-respect, not as barriers to connection.

Yet, this transformation is ongoing. Old fears and patterns may resurface, especially in new or challenging contexts. The journey requires patience, self-awareness, and sometimes support. But with practice, the ease and freedom of living your truth outweigh the discomfort of change.

In the next segment, we will explore how external relationships respond to your evolving no, how people may resist, adapt, or transform alongside you, and how to navigate these dynamics with grace.

The Dance of Resistance and Growth

As your internal landscape shifts and you begin to embody your no with greater confidence and clarity, the external world inevitably responds. Relationships, long accustomed to your automatic yes, may experience disruption. This disruption often unfolds as resistance, confusion, or even conflict, as others adjust to the new boundaries you're setting.

People's reactions vary widely. Some respond with surprise or disappointment, struggling to reconcile the new you with the person they've known. Others may resist more actively, testing your limits with guilt, pressure, or passive-aggressive tactics. This resistance can be painful and unsettling, triggering old fears and doubts.

It's essential to recognize that these responses are less about you and more about the other person's adaptation process. You're no challenge to the familiar script they have relied on, forcing them to reconsider their expectations and behaviors. This recalibration takes time and often stirs discomfort.

In healthy relationships, this disruption becomes an opportunity for growth. When you hold firm with kindness and consistency, you invite more profound honesty and mutual respect. The relationship evolves beyond codependency into authentic connection, where both parties feel seen and honored.

Sometimes, the process reveals misalignments. Relationships that thrived on your silence or compliance may falter. While difficult, this separation can be liberating, clearing space for connections that support your true self.

Navigating these dynamics requires emotional resilience and clear communication. Affirm your boundaries calmly, acknowledge others' feelings without capitulating, and maintain your commitment to your truth.

It also helps to cultivate support networks, friends, mentors, or communities who affirm your journey and provide perspective when resistance feels overwhelming.

Over time, as your no becomes steady and expected, resistance lessens. People learn to respect your boundaries, and your relationships stabilize in new, healthier forms.

This dance between resistance and growth is a natural part of transformation. Embracing it with compassion, toward yourself and others, allows your no to ripple outward, reshaping not only your life but the ecosystem of your relationships.

In the next segment, we will explore affirmations and anchoring practices that support your ability to hold your ground and embody your no with confidence.

Anchoring Your No

Saying no is an act of courage, and courage requires reinforcement. To hold your boundaries with confidence, especially when faced with doubt, guilt, or pushback, it is essential to cultivate inner anchors, affirmations, and practices that root you in your truth and steady your resolve.

Affirmations are powerful tools for rewiring your mindset and reinforcing your self-worth. Simple, clear statements such as "My needs matter," "I have the right to say no," and "Setting boundaries honors my well-being" serve as daily reminders that your no is valid and necessary. Repeating these affirmations, especially in moments of wavering, strengthens the neural pathways associated with self-respect and boundary-setting.

Beyond verbal affirmations, physical practices can ground you in your body's wisdom. Breathwork, for example, calms the nervous system and centers your awareness in the present moment. Slow, deep breaths before and during boundary conversations can ease anxiety and enhance clarity.

Visualization is another effective method. Imagining yourself speaking your no with calm confidence, surrounded by a protective light or supportive presence, prepares your mind and body to embody that state in real situations. This mental rehearsal builds muscle memory, making your response more natural and less reactive.

Journaling offers space to explore fears and resistance that arise around saying no. Writing about your experiences, reflecting on your growth, and articulating your values deepens self-awareness and commitment. It also externalizes internal dialogue, allowing for greater objectivity and compassion.

Creating rituals that affirm your boundaries, such as lighting a candle, placing a meaningful object on your desk, or reciting your affirmations each morning, can embed these practices into your daily life, providing consistent reminders of your commitment.

Importantly, these tools are not about perfection but about progress. There will be moments of challenge, slip-ups, or second-guessing. Anchoring practices support resilience, helping you return to your boundaries with renewed strength.

As you develop these internal supports, your no becomes not a point of contention but a place of power, a sacred act of self-care and clarity.

In the final segment of this chapter, we will reflect on the ongoing journey of empowered decision-making and how embracing your no can open doors to unexpected growth and fulfillment.

The Journey Forward

The decision to say no is not a destination but a beginning, a gateway into a richer, more authentic life. With each no, you step more fully into your power and purpose. This journey invites patience, self-compassion, and courage, as it often challenges long-held beliefs and patterns.

Embracing your no opens space for unexpected growth. It can illuminate new paths, spark creative solutions, and invite deeper relationships founded on honesty rather than obligation. As your boundaries take root, you may find clarity in your goals and alignment in your actions that once felt elusive.

The path is rarely linear. There will be moments of doubt, regression, or resistance from yourself or others. These are opportunities for learning rather than failure. Each time you return to your boundary with resolve, you strengthen your capacity to live with integrity.

Importantly, your no is an invitation to self-respect. It teaches others how to treat you and sets the tone for all your interactions. Living in this way cultivates a life where you can say yes to what truly matters without losing yourself.

As you continue this work, remember to honor your progress. Celebrate each boundary set, each moment of clarity, each experience of courage. These milestones mark your growth and resilience.

The ripple of your no extends beyond your immediate sphere, inspiring those around you to examine their boundaries and embrace their worth.

Transformation through saying no is powerful, but true freedom comes when these changes become part of your daily life. In the final chapter, we'll explore how to maintain your boundaries over time, building habits, systems, and environments that support a boundaried, authentic life.

In the final chapter, we will explore how to make this empowered, boundaried life sustainable, building habits, environments, and support systems that nurture your continued growth and freedom.

Chapter 12: Building a Foundation

Making Boundaries a Lifelong Practice

The journey of setting boundaries is transformative, but sustaining that transformation requires intention, consistency, and flexibility. Living a boundaried life is not a one-time achievement but an ongoing practice woven into the fabric of your days, relationships, and self-care.

Building a foundation for lifelong boundaries begins with acceptance: boundaries will need revisiting, adapting, and reaffirming as your life evolves. What served you in one season may require recalibration in the next. Embracing this fluidity prevents rigidity and invites compassion for yourself during inevitable slips or challenges.

Consistency is the backbone of boundary maintenance. Regularly checking in with yourself, through reflection, journaling, or conversations with trusted confidants, helps you stay aligned with your needs and values. These check-ins allow you to identify when boundaries are slipping, when external pressures are mounting, or when your internal signals are asking for recalibration.

Creating systems to support your boundaries is equally vital. This might include calendars that honor your non-negotiable time, communication templates for difficult conversations, or cultivating a "no-friendly" environment, surrounding yourself with people and cultures that respect your limits and encourage your growth.

When boundaries are breached by others or yourself, recovery without shame is crucial. Slips are natural, not failures. Approaching these moments with curiosity and kindness allows you to learn, adjust, and recommit without harsh self-judgment.

Setting boundaries also means being willing to disappoint others. This truth is often the most difficult to accept. Yet, choosing not to abandon yourself, even if it means others are displeased, is a profound act of self-love and authenticity.

Over time, living with clear boundaries reshapes your relationships and environment. People learn to respect your limits, systems shift to accommodate your needs, and you cultivate resilience that supports your freedom.

This chapter will guide you through tools, rituals, and mindsets that make boundary-setting sustainable, inviting you into a life where your no is a source of strength, clarity, and liberation.

In the next segment, we will explore practical strategies for recovering from boundary slips and cultivating a culture of respect and support around your limits.

Recovery and Resilience

Living a boundaried life is a continuous practice, and like all practices, it includes moments of challenge, missteps, and slips. Boundaries are not rigid walls but living, breathing lines that sometimes blur or falter. When you experience a boundary slip, whether it's saying yes when you meant no, overcommitting, or allowing others to overstep, it's vital to approach the moment with self-compassion rather than shame.

Recovery begins with acknowledgment. Recognize what happened without judgment. This clarity is essential to understanding the patterns or triggers that led to the slip. Did fatigue dull your resolve? Did guilt pressure you into compliance? Did an unexpected situation catch you unprepared? Next, reflect on the impact of the slip. How did it affect your energy, your stress levels, your relationships? This honest appraisal reinforces the importance of boundaries and helps motivate recommitment.

Recommitting to your boundaries involves forgiving yourself and setting a clear intention to restore your limits. It may also include communicating openly with others if a boundary breach affected them, offering transparency without over-apologizing.

Building resilience around boundary maintenance is about learning from these moments and equipping yourself with tools to prevent similar slips. This could be rehearsing difficult conversations, strengthening your internal affirmations, or establishing clearer systems for saying no.

Cultivating a culture of support is equally important. Surround yourself with people who respect your limits and encourage your growth. Engage with communities or mentors who understand the journey and can provide accountability and encouragement.

Creating "no-friendly" environments extends beyond relationships. It includes your workspace, digital life, and daily routines. Setting up reminders, using boundary-affirming language in communications, and designing spaces that honor your needs all contribute to sustaining your practice.

Remember, boundary-setting is an act of liberation, not punishment. Each recovery strengthens your self-trust and deepens your capacity to live authentically.

In the next segment, we will explore tools for ongoing boundary check-ins, simple but powerful practices to keep your boundaries vibrant and responsive as your life unfolds.

The Power of Check-Ins

Maintaining boundaries is an ongoing process, requiring regular attention and recalibration. Without intentional check-ins, boundaries can become blurred, outdated, or forgotten amid life's shifting demands. Establishing consistent rituals for reflecting on your limits ensures that your boundaries remain vibrant, aligned, and responsive to your evolving needs.

Monthly or quarterly boundary audits offer a structured opportunity to assess what's working and what isn't. During these check-ins, reflect on questions like: Which boundaries have been respected? Where have you felt pressure to compromise? Are your current commitments aligned with your values and energy? What adjustments do you need to make?

These reflections can be recorded in a journal or digital document, creating a living record of your boundary journey. Over time, this archive reveals patterns and progress, offering insight and motivation.

Daily or weekly mini check-ins are also valuable. Taking a few moments to pause and ask yourself, "How am I feeling about my boundaries today?" or "What do I need to say no to this week to protect my wellbeing?" keeps your limits top of mind and supports proactive boundary-setting.

Sharing your check-in intentions with trusted friends, mentors, or support groups can enhance accountability and deepen your commitment. Knowing that others hold space for your boundaries reinforces your resolve and encourages you during challenging times.

Integrating boundary awareness into your planning practices, whether through calendar notes, to-do list reminders, or habit trackers, transforms boundary maintenance from abstract intention into concrete action.

Remember, these check-ins are not about perfection or rigidity but about curiosity and responsiveness. Boundaries must evolve as you grow and your life changes. Being willing to adapt and release outdated limits is part of sustaining a healthy, boundaried life.

In this way, boundary check-ins become acts of self-care and self-respect, nurturing your autonomy and freedom.

In the final segment, we will reflect on the journey you've undertaken through this book, affirm the power of your no, and offer encouragement for the boundaried life ahead.

Your Life, Your No

As you reach the culmination of this journey, pause to acknowledge how far you have come. Saying no is not just a skill; it is a profound act of reclaiming your life, your time, your energy, your boundaries, and ultimately, your freedom. It is a declaration that you will no longer live by default or for others' expectations, but by choice and authenticity.

Living a boundaried life is an ongoing dance, a balance of firmness and flexibility, strength and compassion, clarity and kindness. It asks you to take up space unapologetically, to honor your needs even when it means disappointing others, and to trust that your yeses will be all the more potent for the no's you have cultivated.

This life invites you to see it not as a denial, but as a sacred decision, a portal to deeper alignment with who you truly are. Each "no" creates space for joy, creativity, rest, and genuine, nourishing connection.

Remember that boundaries are not barriers but bridges, bridges that connect you to yourself and others with honesty and respect. They are invitations for relationships to flourish in truth rather than sacrifice.

Your journey will continue beyond these pages, with new challenges, growth, and discoveries. There will be moments of doubt and discomfort, but also moments of clarity and liberation. Carry the tools, affirmations, and practices you have learned as companions on your path.

Celebrate your courage. Trust your voice. Embrace your freedom.

Your life is yours again.

About the Author

Sage Monroe is a writer, coach, and advocate specializing in personal empowerment and emotional well-being. With over a decade of experience guiding individuals to reclaim their time and voice, Sage blends practical strategies with compassionate insight to help readers break free from people-pleasing patterns and set healthy boundaries. When not writing or coaching, Sage enjoys hiking, meditation, and exploring the art of mindful living.

About the Publisher

Welcome to The Book On Publishing

At The Book On Publishing, we believe in rewriting the rules of learning. Whether you're chasing your next big idea, building a better life, or simply curious about what should have been taught in school, you've come to the right place.

We're a platform built for dreamers, doers, and lifelong learners, offering bold, practical books and tools that empower you to take charge of your journey. From real-world skills to mindset mastery, we publish the book on what matters.

No fluff. No lectures. Just what you need to know, delivered with clarity, purpose, and a spark of curiosity.

Start exploring. Start growing. Start writing your story.

Read more at https://thebookon.ca.

Acknowledgment of AI Assistance

Portions of this book were developed with the support of ChatGPT, an AI language model created by OpenAI. While every word has been carefully reviewed and refined by the author, ChatGPT served as a valuable tool for brainstorming, editing, and structuring ideas. Its assistance helped accelerate the creative process and bring clarity to complex topics.

www.ingramcontent.com/pod-product-compliance
Lightning Source LLC
Chambersburg PA
CBHW071739120626
46550CB00002B/584